THE LITTLE
SILVER
BOOK™

INTERVIEWING

Everything You Need to Know

T0204509

D. NEIL BERDIEV

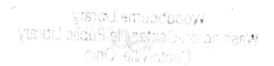

Copyright © 2014 D. Neil Berdiev

Published by D. Neil Berdiev, DNB Advisory, Boston, MA

First edition, September 2014
ISBN: 0977411737
ISBN 13: 9780977411733

Library of Congress Control Number: 2014911403
DNB Advisory, Boston, MA

Table of Contents

~

Table of Contents

Every little situation presents many
lessons and experiences.
The question is: what will *you* learn from them,
and *how* will you use them to your advantage?

With Gratitude

~

To Dina, Chapa, and Tauri: it's the little, tiny moments that matter the most.

To people who miss the interview mark and especially the clueless ones, for without you this book would have no place and no purpose.

To those who have been forgiving of my own interview mishaps and failures and who gave me a chance on some jobs.

To those who excel in interviews, because hiring teams would not want to do their jobs without you and without a glimpse of hope from you that all is not lost.

To those nay-sayers who kept reminding me that a book like this would not be useful. Without you I would not have been able to make this book a reality.

What Inspired This Book

~

I first came to the United States in my late teens, from a small country called Turkmenistan. Most people I meet tell me they have never heard of it before. I was remarkably oblivious to the ways of the labor market in this country and the various aspects of job hunting. In a way, my situation was similar to those of high school and undergraduate students before they obtain relevant knowledge of career development strategies.

In my home country, back in the 1990s and before that (I don't know how it is now); most decent jobs were distributed through family or friends' connections or through bribes. You could apply for a position all you wanted to, but your capabilities did not determine the outcome. It was very frustrating to apply for jobs. My father, who held a high position in the government, never helped me, and he was against nepotism and bribes. Although I did not appreciate it then, it was a life lesson in disguise: you have to rely on yourself to get you where you need to go. Someday your family and friends might not be there for you. However, the experience you gain will continue to drive your success or failure.

While I eventually figured out how to tackle the job search in the United States and learned to do it quite well, the first couple of years were really tough. I interviewed for many jobs – some that I was clearly qualified for. Alas, I did not get any of them. I had to settle for work as a waiter and on bartending gigs, which in retrospect were terrific experiences. They gave me skills that were directly transferrable to the corporate world, and aided my success (but that is another story.)

Still, career development and the interview skills that are part of it require constant work and improvement. It's never easy. In part, this is because our career growth leads to greater challenges than just getting that first job. There is a lot of information available on the Internet, in books, and through other sources. The challenge is distilling this knowledge into what's actually useful. Anybody who's a nobody who wants to be a somebody is sharing advice on how to interview and professing that you can learn to do it in thirty minutes and five steps. External recruiters claim that they are the path to job offers. Yet, few of them know what they are doing, and even fewer care about you and your future. For them, it's just a job and a stepping stone to something greater.

There needs to be something better than the current barrage of useless information that is far from reality. This is one of the reasons I wrote this book, and my hope is that it will be a stepping stone in the right direction, giving you the skills to think for yourself.

Introduction

~

Interviewing is an experience like no other: it is a sales pitch, a marketing dance, a courting ceremony, an elimination game, a ritual, a negotiation process, a high-stakes affair, a speed date, and an investigation – all in one. Some interviews are fast and furious. Others are protracted and seem to be never-ending. Ultimately, they lead to some people winning and others losing, both interviewers and interviewees.

Many books, articles, and training programs have been created to educate job hunters on how to interview. Schools, colleges, and universities coach students on how to master the art of interviewing. Some even make resume writing and interviewing part of their required curriculum. Coaches and consultants dedicate countless hours to bestowing their interviewing expertise upon job seekers.

Yet hiring managers continue to be exasperated over the fact that so many applicants fail everything, from the very elementary must-haves to more sophisticated expectations.

After many years of interviewing and interviews with hundreds of candidates, I think it is obvious that interviews can but do not always uncover your technical, interpersonal, problem-solving, and other skills. Rather, they are a preview or the lifting of a stage curtain for a quick glimpse of what's likely to come. Interviewers assemble the rest of your profile by the method of deduction. A part of this quick unveiling contains many obvious and subtle rules, expectations, and etiquette. This book is your chance to understand the game and to help you focus interviewers on your true qualities.

FUNDAMENTALS

1

You Get One Chance – Make It Count!

~

Before you learn about interviewing and how to do it well, think of the interview process as an elimination game. You get one chance only! All too often interviewees do not invest enough time and effort to prepare for the interview and to interview seriously. Unless you are interviewing at someone's insistence and your primary goal is to do everything possible to botch your interview, why waste your time and other people's time applying? Don't enter the playing field unless you are prepared to play to win.

Think of the interview process as a framework with three distinct components:

- before the interview,
- during the interview, and
- after the interview.

3

Each of the three steps presents a set of challenges and opportunities. Each requires specific knowledge to tackle it successfully. Also, look at your entire career as one ongoing interview process. As you will see in the chapters that follow, certain interviewing qualities develop and become polished over extended periods of time. In real life there is no magic pill, hugely popular "five or ten tips on …" article, or a substitute for real, hands-on experience. The sooner you start, the more benefits you will reap by polishing your interviewing and career development skills.

Lastly, draw a map to visualize the three interviewing phases. For each phase, determine your true strengths so you can capitalize on them and select one or two weaknesses so you can minimize their impact, particularly if they could be stumbling blocks that might knock you out of the running. *More on this exercise is in the Bonus section at the end.*

2
The Black Hole of Recruiting

~

If you have already applied for several positions, you know that the recruiting process can be a black hole of inconsistency, unresponsiveness, and lack of basic awareness of what is going on. You are never in the driver's seat when you are flushing your resume into an "application portal." This does not mean that you have zero chances of getting a job. Still, the chances are low unless your skills and experiences are something that your future employer is wowed by. But that's not the situation for many of us.

You can, however, gain a competitive advantage by understanding how organizations work and by developing a network. This network can help you maneuver through the application labyrinth. The only thing that many qualified applicants need is to be noticed by recruiters and for hiring managers to have a few extra seconds to appreciate them. That fair chance can come from having a connection on the inside.

It is critical to understand the following:
- what specific needs and challenges the hiring team is trying to solve by filling the vacancy;
- what hiring managers are looking for;
- what her or his vision is for the group and for the job;
- what the application time frame is;
- where a company is in the hiring process; and
- what the interviewing and decision-making process is.

If you have these covered, your candidacy will have a fighting chance. You can move past resumes that get overlooked due to the lack of resources, portals that do not even deliver resumes, and a deluge of other applicants.

3
Networking Is Not About Numbers

Despite the instant nature of LinkedIn, Facebook, Twitter, and various other social networks, real networks take time to build. Real networks are not a numbers game. If you have greater than five hundred contacts on LinkedIn, it does not mean that those people will give you the time of day or help you maneuver toward a career opportunity. What you need for a successful application bid is a network that can offer access to information, support, and brutally honest advice.

Here are several tips to help you develop a strong, relationship-based network that will help you with your career moves:

- If you need assistance when applying for a job, be honest with people and don't try to make it look like networking.

- Be respectful of people's time and don't waste it.
- Networking may require growing a thick skin and pushing beyond your comfort zone.
- The majority of people will respond positively to a networking request if you have tact and finesse when approaching them.
- Develop and grow your network before you need people's help.
- Networking is a never-ending process.
- Stay in contact with key people, or your network will be nothing more than a one-hit wonder.
- Think of ways to add value to your network members and pay it forward.

In general, it takes six to twelve months to lay a good foundation for successful networking in a particular company or industry. Start early! See *the bonus article at the end of this book on developing high-quality professional networks.*

4
Is This the Best You've Got?

~

Interviewing is presenting yourself in the best possible light to your prospective employers. Every hiring manager and recruiter expects this. Naturally, she or he wants to see the real you. Part of the challenge for some interviewees is figuring out who they are, because only then can they deliver a clear message about themselves. That's something you will need to sort out before applying anywhere. If a hiring team fails to uncover who you are and what you stand for, they risk having the problem of an underperforming employee to deal with later on.

Future employers also expect that in the very brief period of time during which they interact with you, in person or electronically, you will deliver your very best performance. I hear this year after year from hiring teams: if you can't even do your best and exhibit your best behavior while applying for the job, how are you going to perform on it, when it requires commitment and results day after day? Or, if you can't be on your best behavior now, what should we expect when you are hired? They will interpret subpar performance as a lack of drive, stamina, and ability to get the job done.

Thus, the best way to tackle every application is to demonstrate that you are not only good for the job while applying for it, but also that the employer can be confident that you will deliver a top performance if you are hired. Interviews are sprints, and jobs are marathons. Can you be versatile enough for both?

5
Business Writing Skills are Priceless

Before you get to talk to anyone on a hiring team, you will likely be corresponding with her or him in writing. Research, comments from managers, and annual multi-billion-dollar corporate expenditures on business writing show that writing skills have become an endangered "species." Our texting and messaging lifestyle is one of the key reasons why we can't write. Yet it is not an excuse for poor writing skills when you are applying for a job. In today's competitive environment, especially for candidates with limited to no experience, hiring managers make decisions within the first ten to thirty seconds about whether they'd like to speak with you or not. The quality of your business writing is critical to those impressions.

Applicants are rejected for many reasons. They may not have known the conventions of how to properly address a person they are writing to, may have made a typo that went uncorrected, or might not have wrapped up the message with a proper, respectful closing. Yes, the reality is commonly just as simple as that. Look at this as your rite of passage. If you do not pass the written "test," you may not move to the next step. Employers aren't interested in hiring people who are unable to write well, effectively, and in a results-oriented way.

- First and foremost, assume that your business writing skills are not adequate.
- Second, have someone who writes well critique your writing – from emails and business communications to your cover letter and other written work.
- Third, pour through your work multiple times in search of typos, grammatical and punctuation errors, lengthy and run-on sentences, and anything else that may not pass the demanding eye of a business writer.
- Finally, the only way to get better is through practice.

6
Attention to Detail Is Everything

~

Even the most creative jobs require attention to detail – some much more than others. When reviewing a candidate's resume, cover letter, appearance, body language, speech, and many other elements, prospective employers pay close attention to details.

Let's say that you move into a brand new house from an old apartment. Everything seems to be high-end at first. Once you get adjusted to the new surroundings, you begin to notice that outlets are installed without proper leveling and at different heights and positions relative to one another. You spot that some door handles are gold-colored and others are silver. The floor in a couple of areas is not leveled, and when a ball is dropped it rolls off to one side. If you bought the house and then noticed all the defects, you would be very upset to have bought a lemon.

The recruiting process is very similar. A good recruiter or a hiring manager is like a good home inspector: her or his job is to identify issues, flaws, and lack of attention to detail. Experienced interviewers can pick up on the lack of attention to detail on the spot because they interview often. Once they detect it, they move on to the next candidate.

You might not have brought along multiple copies of your resume. You might have forgotten a pen or an extra pen in case the first one stopped working. You might not have thanked the interviewer for her or his consideration. You might have forgotten to ask for a business card or to follow up with a thank you note. Or you might not have pressed your shirt or cleaned and shined your shoes. To an interviewer, lack of attention to detail may signal the difference between success and failure, especially if details are essential to successful performance.

7
The Power of a Notepad

~

Mistake #1: Many job seekers forget to have a notepad and a pen with them at all times. As tablets become more and more widespread, they begin to serve the purpose of note pads. Mistake #2: Job applicants forget or do not want to take notes. Why do you bring along a notepad if you just keep it as a stale accessory? The application process is not a fashion show. Mistake #3: Many fail to act or follow up on the information captured in notes.

Avoiding these mistakes is essential for a successful professional, but it all starts with a simple notepad.

There is nothing more frustrating for an interviewer than an applicant receiving valuable information and letting it go in one ear and right out the other. What your actions say is that you are willing to waste someone else's time. Additionally, you do not have to be face-to-face for interviewers to know that you had no takeaways. If you do not follow up on the information you received, the interviewer concludes that you are either disorganized or did not take notes. Either can be ruinous to your chances of securing a job.

You may ask why a person would want to write anything down with so much technology at their disposal. Typing and clicking is distracting, disrespectful, and requires focusing away from the conversation. Further, no interviewer will consent to a recording. Note-taking is still a reliable way to get the job done.

Remember that valuable information can and will come at you at any point, and it will sometimes come when you do not expect it. Having a note pad, taking notes, and following up on those notes is what successful interviewees do and what employers expect.

8

I'm Like, You're Like, and We're Like...

~

It is time to recognize that the majority of us have lost the ability to speak well. I am not referring to some type of superficial, pompous conversation. How about a simple ability to speak grammatically correct sentences in a fluid way, without filler words and phrases, such as "like," "hmmm," "aaahhh," "you know what I mean," "in essence," and others? They permeate almost every sentence in a conversation. For recruiting teams, such speech is an "earsore" that stands out and not in a good way.

A hiring manager will quickly tune you out if you allow these speech deficiencies to come through. The reaction will range from viewing you as immature and "green" (even if you are an experienced candidate), to having a fear of putting you in front of colleagues and especially in front of clients.

For those who can't switch quickly enough from colloquial, daily speech with family and friends to a more formal, better quality speaking ability, you may have to force yourself to speak in a "proper" manner at all times. For those who are capable of switching back and forth from "I'm like" and "you know what I mean" to what's expected during interviews, make sure that you still practice enough to develop a sense of confidence. Do not let your social environment derail your chances of getting a job you want.

Action points:
- Have a partner record, count, and point out how many times you use filler works, make grammatical mistakes, and speak with flaws.
- Learn to listen to yourself and correct your language.

9

All Eyes Are on You

~

During any interview process, you have lots of eyes on you. In a way, you are under a microscope. An experienced hiring team has a way of dissecting your candidacy under a variety of angles. Depending on what the job entails and the type of candidate sought, businesses evaluate both a formal and informal range of qualities. If they were to build a checklist, it might look like the list below.

You need to meet the majority – if not all – of the criteria with flying colors to get a job. Additionally, the quality of other candidates will influence this evaluation, and you may be graded on a curve, depending on how the other candidates perform.

- Cover letter and resume quality
- Preliminary communications with the candidate

- Verbal communication skills on the phone
- Degree to which the person's experiences and prior accomplishments qualify her or him for the job (*could be a separate checklist with various qualities and requirements*)
- Possession of licenses and certifications that may be required for the job
- Successfully passing a case study or other assessment tools as part of the interview process
- Energy level throughout the process
- Interview results
- Appearance
- Verbal communication skills
- Behavior
- Ability to interact well with other interviewees and members of the hiring team
- Salary expectations versus what the company would like to pay
- Ability to fit on the team
- Ability to reach the required goals
- Extent to which the candidate really wants the job
- Future career aspirations
- Post-interview communications
- Ability to write
- Hiring team vote and stack-ranking
- Informal, behind-the-scenes references and inquiries
- Formal background checks as condition to employment

The above is a high-level checklist. The actual criteria may be more detailed and extensive. Some elements that go into the decision-making process are quantifiable and fairly objective, but many are subjective. This makes the selection process a non-scientific, human-influenced assessment where the candidates who are most qualified (from a technical perspective) do not always get the job.

This is why it is very important to understand all the key expectations, know your strengths and weaknesses, and learn to recognize and fix what is likely to hurt you as a candidate. As we say in the commercial banking industry when we refer to credit analysis: credit analysis is part art and part science. It is at the intersection of the two where commercial banks finance businesses. Similarly, interviewing is just as much an art as it is a science. Learning to master the various elements of interviewing can pay hefty dividends.

BEFORE THE INTERVIEW

10

Building Image from the First Impression

~

Everything you do from the moment you apply for a vacancy (and even long before that) creates your personal image or brand, whether strong or weak, positive or negative. Your energy and your attitude are a significant part of how you are perceived. A big turnoff for recruiters is individuals who are low on energy or who come across as being too casual. The former can be interpreted as a lack of drive. The latter can be interpreted as a lack of propriety and respect.

While we all have different personalities, most hiring teams are enamored with energy, enthusiasm, and respectful attitude. A high energy level is typically indicative of your drive toward performance. Energetic individuals tend to be driven and self-motivated, and they can bring a positive charge into their teams. Your energy and how you carry yourself matters!

Interviewers also want to see whether you can conduct yourself professionally, even if you are a laid-back, relaxed individual. They want to know if: a) you can switch gears quickly to exude a professional demeanor, and b) you are able to stand in front of clients and business partners and be professional and respectful.

Action points:
- Practice in front of a mirror or with a friend to gather feedback on whether you are an energetic person and how you can improve your energy when low.
- Ask for feedback from people outside your circle to assess your level of professionalism.

11
Hey, Hey, Hey

~

Many interviewees, especially the younger ones, tend to forget that interviewers are not their buddies or family members. Even if you have a very engaging conversation with a hiring manager, it does not mean that you are friends for life. Some of this is about knowing your audience and about using proper behavior. In many industries it is not acceptable to send a communication that opens with a "Hey". The "hey" option may not be acceptable at all when dealing with more senior colleagues and definitely not while interviewing for a job. It is a matter of being respectful and being formal.

Hiring teams will interpret your "hey" as a lack of maturity, etiquette, or flat-out unprofessional behavior that is not suitable in business settings. This does not mean that you can't be yourself and relaxed when you interview. Being yourself allows you to be successful in interacting with others. Yet, it is different from not knowing when and how to behave.

An example of "hey" taken to the next level is the greeting of "Hey, what's up, dude?" that came from a just-out-of-college hire addressing a team leader who was walking toward him in a hallway. To say that the greeting was not received well would be a gross understatement. It was followed by: "Come to my office. We need to talk."

Action points:
- Do not use "hey" or other casual speech during interviews (verbal or written communications).
- Err on the side of caution, even if you get the job, unless informal behavior is welcome in that company.
- Even if it is acceptable, not every person appreciates casual treatment. Know your audience!

12
This Scheduling Is Painful Business

~

One way to kill your chances of getting a job is to make it extremely difficult to set up an interview. Unless you are a hot employee commodity, you will usually find yourself in a buyer's market. Employers have the ultimate say about whether they want you. This means that if you want a shot at getting an offer, you should be as accommodating as you can be. Nobody cares if you have a packed school calendar or many responsibilities that keep you working 24-7 in your current role. Do you want the job or not?

You have to realize that the hiring team will need to meet with many candidates. Scheduling its various team members to meet with even one person is already a logistical nightmare. If you can't help the team by being accommodating and flexible, they will question if you really want the job. The hiring team may also wonder if the scheduling difficulty is a glimpse into your inflexible nature and your inability to adapt quickly to changing circumstances. In this competitive labor environment, successful employees are highly flexible and nimble. Everyone else gets left behind.

One last tip: make sure that each time you turn down a proposed interview time, you offer alternative dates. This will cut down on the number of back-and-forth e-mails and will make scheduling more collaborative.

Action points:
- Be as flexible as possible when scheduling interview- related meetings. Chances are that you need the job, not them.
- If you have limited to no availability to meet over a certain period of time, think twice about whether or not now is a good time to look for a job.

13
Firing in All Directions

~

If quantity is the hallmark of your job-hunting strategy, make sure that you are hyper-organized in tracking inquiries, cover letters, resumes, and follow-up communications. Otherwise you risk referring to one employer by its competitor's name or calling Mr. Smith, Ms. Johnson.

Volume strategy has its place, although it can take a lot longer than an approach focused on building lasting, quality relationships. Here are examples of when a volume search may work: when you need a job now; when you have limited periods of time to search consistently; or when the labor market is so competitive that you choose to play a numbers game just to get in the door to as many companies as possible.

If you choose to flood the market with your applications, have a detailed, painstakingly organized system that tracks everything, including follow-up items and responses you receive. If you fail in any of these steps, you may find yourself in the position of one applicant: he reached out to a hiring manager via LinkedIn to speak about a job opportunity, and they set a time to talk. He then sent another message three days later to the same person, introducing himself and asking for a brief conversation. His excuse was that "LinkedIn must be sending automatic messages." As you might guess, the scheduled conversation never took place. Who needs a disorganized employee who can't take responsibility for a screw-up?

Action points:
- Be extremely organized with all phases of your job search.
- Take the time to personalize your messages for each occurrence.

14
Dear Sirs

~

If you live in the twenty-first century – and chances are that you do – using the greeting "Dear Sirs" can send your cover letter or an e-mail straight into a recycling bin. The reader does not need to be a woman to take offense. Many men are progressive enough to have a strong reaction to this archaic, sexist salutation.

At a minimum, your greeting should be "Dear Sir or Madam." You can be more progressive by writing "Dear Madam or Sir." "To Whom It May Concern," to many hiring managers, means that it does not concern them at all. You can be more personal if you are able to find the right person to address your correspondence to; however, do not pester them or disregard requests such as "Do not call." Think of dozens, if not hundreds, of applicants starting their communications with plain, generic, and impersonal salutations. It is never too early to stand out from other contenders.

Your goal should be to determine who the point of contact is so that you can send your resume to someone more than an impersonal addressee in the black hole of resume submissions. That means that unless the name of the recruiter is provided, you need to have a strong enough network to find out who it is.

Action points:
- Find out the name of the person to whom you should submit your resume as opposed to using impersonal salutations.
- Proper salutation is just the beginning of demonstrating to the reader that you actually know how to write well.
- The proper, formal way is to have a colon after the salutation, not a comma.

15

Cover Letters Can Be a Painful Business

~

Cover letters can take many shapes and forms. They range from a traditional cover letter to express your interest in an opportunity to a simple e-mail to inquire about an opening. While cover letters are not typically required anymore, they are useful for many reasons: they can explain why you are the best candidate for a job; they can highlight your key experiences; and they can do what a resume can't by helping you stand out from an ocean of resumes, if written well.

Although many books and articles about cover letters have been published, it is remarkable how few people do them right. The most common failures include the following:

- They are extremely lengthy and tend to lose the reader.
- They look like too much of a generic template – not focused on what the company is looking for.
- They lack the proper structure: an opening, why you are interested in the opportunity, what you offer, why you are a high-quality candidate, and a concluding statement thanking the reader for her or his consideration.
- They are filled with typos, grammatical errors, lengthy sentences, or just hard-to-follow language.

Instead of focusing on getting you to the interview, flawed cover letters attempt to "interview" on your behalf. This means that you are missing the whole point of the cover letter: in a concise way, entice the reader's interest in your candidacy to get you to an interview so that you can then close the deal.

Action point:
- Make your cover letter help you get pulled out of the black hole of resumes and make it interesting enough so that potential employers would want to meet to learn more.

16
False Pretenses

~

If you are an entrepreneurial job seeker, I want to caution you against taking your creativity to the next level. Never pretend that you want to learn about a company (or something else) when your intent is to apply for a job. Starting a relationship with a lie can come back to haunt you.

Many people are willing to help a fellow alum or a network member learn about a company or industry. Yet they do not like to be used and then discover that your interest was just a cover to help you move your resume to the top of the pile. The fallout can be more devastating if the person you reach out to is the hiring manager. The recruiting cycle is typically finite once a requisition is created. As a consequence, you can't take your time to develop a relationship with a center of influence, and your real intention will come out quickly enough.

Even if you are truly interested in learning more, the risk of appearing deceptive is far too great to a relationship that could be more impactful to your career in the long term. You have to make a choice whether to continue developing the connection or applying for the job, in which case you risk undoing all the good that may have come from meeting this individual. Always think long-term!

Action points:
- Choose whether you want to develop a network or apply for a job – but not both.
- Business relationships have to be built on honesty and trust. This is not just a cliché.
- If your contact suggests that you apply for a specific job, you are in the clear.

17

This Mailbox Is Full

Let's suppose for a moment that you are a recruiter or a hiring manager and would like to follow up with an applicant who piqued your interest. You send an e-mail or want to leave a voice mail for this individual to schedule time to talk, and you get: "This voice mail box is full" or "This e-mail inbox is full."

What does this tell you about the person, especially when compared to other contenders? The conclusions will likely include: this person is not in charge, is clueless, does not want people to contact her or him, and does not know how to use communication tools well enough to deserve the job. A wackier recruiter with a vivid imagination might attribute this to being on the run from the Feds or hiding from debt collectors. Whatever your wild guesses might be, they will not be favorable, and you will move on to the next person on the list. Remember that hiring teams are too busy to waste their time on guessing games.

Think about the first impression you make – an impression that can be a deciding factor in favor of other people. Also, remember that a first impression is a conclusion about your *attention to detail.* Attention to detail is everything. These situations arise a lot more frequently than you'd think. In a way, it helps an under-resourced individual in a screening or hiring role get to the right candidate faster. And making a negative first impression is so easily preventable.

Action points:
- Make sure that you check your e-mail or voice mail boxes for adequate space.
- Create a polished greeting for your voice mail.
- Check your messages frequently to prevent the shutdown of your inbox.

18
You Have Reached (617)-_-_

~

One of the first steps in orienting or on-boarding new employees to high-performing teams is instructing them how to set up their voice mail boxes and e-mail signatures. The goal is for everyone to project a high-quality professional image. While nobody requires an applicant to have the same voice mail and e-mail inbox set up that you'd encounter in a sophisticated company, professionalism is always appreciated and valued. That's what makes you stand out.

Suppose you are the hiring manager, calling a prospective applicant to schedule an interview. After dialing, you hear: "You have reached 617-___-____" or just a beep right away, without any identification. You might think that the company does not have the applicant's correct contact information. Yet, there is no time to dwell on it, and you have other applicants to focus on.

Even if you leave a message, the applicant has lost valuable points.

Cute messages push the limits even further and are not likely to be in your favor. A message such as "You know what to do and when to do it" makes your prospective employers think: Yes, I do know what to do. Next applicant, please.

Action points:
- Clear out your mail box and record the kind of professional-sounding, friendly message you'd expect employees of firms where you are applying to have, including a greeting, message content, and wrap-up.
- Consider creating an e-mail signature for your outgoing messages. You should also consider setting up an auto response to incoming messages, especially when you are away for an extended period of time.
- Never answer phone calls with "Yeah" or "What's up."

19

Beachbum@xyz.com

~

Following the theme of exuding *high levels of professionalism, organization,* and *attention to detail,* review the e-mail account you use for job applications. If your e-mail address is something along the lines of *beachbum@xyz. com,* it is time to do something about it. If your target industry or company is all about goofiness, weirdness, or wackiness, then make no changes. Otherwise, create a separate account for career matters. Always know your audience and understand that there is a time and place for play and one for work.

E-mail accounts are free and easy to set up. If you can't be bothered to fix such an easy image item as your e-mail account, the hiring managers will draw conclusions about how much you want the job and whether they want someone like you representing their business. When setting up a new e-mail account, the easiest and the most straight-forward address is one that includes your first and last name. If that combination is already taken, consider adding numbers or other signs to it.

Be aware that longer and obscure e-mail addresses, such as dkm1992spn14@gmail.com, make it harder for hiring teams to type. Thus, you risk causing an error that will make an e-mail intended for you to bounce. Make sure it is as easy as possible for people to enter your e-mail address and contact you.

Action points:
- Create a professional e-mail address and keep your unique views on life out of it, if they are not likely to be appreciated. Also, make your name part of your e-mail address.
- If you can't check this new account address regularly, forward e-mails to your regular account so that you can quickly respond to e-mails that come in.

20
I Know Everything about You

~

In our information age, with easy access to lots of public and non-public data, you must restrain your investigative drive. While there is nothing wrong with being curious about your prospective interviewers and employers, you do not want to come across as having been snooping on them. In matters of privacy, focus on your efforts to apply as opposed to researching your potential employers. Do not behave like a stalker with an unhealthy interest in people's private matters.

LinkedIn is one example of a site where recruiters and hiring managers can view your profile. They also know that you viewed theirs (depending on your settings). Does this mean that you should make a reference to the interviewer's background to demonstrate that you did your research? Perhaps. However, be very careful about bringing it up at all if your communication skills are not strong. Find the right opportunity to bring it up as part of your conversation to build rapport; yet, avoid dwelling on it beyond a cursory reference.

You should limit your research and conversations to matters of professional background. Under no circumstances should you talk about the interviewer's children, place of residence, or any other personal details without an invitation to discuss them. This is a guaranteed way to make the interviewer uncomfortable and lose your chances for the job.

Action points:
- Be incredibly sensitive about researching your potential employers and how you communicate what you learn to them.
- If you find data that questions the integrity and ethics of your prospective colleagues, decide if you want to work with them. Leave them out of your decision-making.

21
Thought We Could Be Best Friends

~

It is remarkable how some individuals overdo the getting-to-know-you part of professional relationship building. Instead, they are eager to jump right ahead to being your best friend. Do not interpret a person's willingness to network or spend time to talk about her or his industry or company as an immediate invitation to become pals. Business should not be mixed with personal friendships – at least not until you have a stronger personal connection. And connections typically take time and numerous interactions to build.

You should not be proactively contacting hiring team members prior to the interview, unless you are given permission to reach out. Also, respect the lines of communication. If a particular HR team member contacts you, maintain contact with that individual. Do not proactively move to her or his colleagues. There is nothing worse for a hiring manager than getting e-mails or calls from a person she or he is scheduled to interview but never had an introduction to. The same rules apply to post-interview contact. Unless you were given explicit consent to contact an individual, limit your contacts to thank-you notes and follow-up inquiries.

Last but certainly not least, interviewers have no desire to be tracked through personal social networks (like Facebook or Qzone) with annoying requests to become friends. You should tame your initiative and go-getter spirit and know what's appropriate.

Action points:
- Keep your business and personal affairs separate.
- Think twice before contacting your interviewers and decide whether they'd want to hear from you.

22
We Turkmen Need to Stick Together!

~

It is common for people to connect with and support members of the same "community." These communities include ethnic groups, industry organizations, or alumni of the same school. Yet, it is nauseating when prospective job seekers have the expectation and even the sense of entitlement that they will be helped because they are a member of the same group.

There are some things you do not need to be reminded of. If an individual supports members of a particular group, she or he does it naturally and is happy to help. Being Turkmen myself, I met for an informational interview with another Turkmen who called me "brother" several times and emphasized that "we Turkmen need to stick together." This kind of expectation of support and these reminders erased any desire I initially had to help a person of the same heritage. The same is true of just about any person you might be affiliated with.

People are inclined to support someone who can stand on their own two feet before anything else – someone who has the intelligence and ability to be successful and only needs some guidance or support. Focus on your strengths as opposed to looking for shortcuts and trying to get success delivered on a silver platter. Successful people who built careers and fortunes on their own merits like people who are out to do the same.

Action points:
- Take advantage of connections with individuals who share background similarities with you. More importantly, take advantage of their advice and guidance.
- Never expect that affiliation with the same group as someone else promises jobs or other perks – you have to earn them!

23
Who the Heck Are You?

~

During your career-search endeavors you will reach out to many unfamiliar people. Some of them may be hiring team members, while others might be people you network with. This can be a hit-or-miss venture. What's important is to have several important expectations and tactics to improve your chances for success. Your ultimate goal is to convert these people into your greatest allies or, at a minimum, people who would want to be on your side.

You will need to develop thick skin to deal with rejection or lack of response, appreciate it tremendously. Expect that some individuals will not respond to your inquiries or invitations to meet. Yet, many will. It is valuable to remember that no one owes you anything. Each time you get a positive response. Bring positive energy and professional friendliness into your communications, and these traits will help you open most doors. However, do not go overboard: develop a balance between being personable but not too casual.

Never fool yourself about what you can offer to those you network with. In many instances it is you who will need assistance and support. See these situations for what they are. Additionally, not all first-time meetings with prospective employers or opportunities to network will lead to great business connections. It is all part of the process. Finally, existing connections can run their course, and only a few will become lifelong contacts. That's okay. When some relationships become part of the past, it may be time to develop new ones.

Action point:

- Have a positive attitude in reaching out to unfamiliar individuals, and many will respond positively.

24
Do Not Misuse Informational Interviews

~

Informational interviews are distinctly different from interviewing to apply for a job. The two have different goals and purposes as well as different etiquette. Informational interviews are similar to meetings for networking. The goal is to learn more about a company or an industry, explore a career track, or develop a valuable connection.

A common error is to ask for an informational interview when you actually intend to apply for a job. When a company is trying to fill a vacancy, hiring managers will not have the time or desire to spend time with people who want to find out if the opportunity is the right fit. The only exception to this rule is when you know someone on the inside very well. This person may talk about the company, the team, and the position proper. Even then, it can be awkward if after an informational interview you turn around and apply for the job.

The ultimate misuse of informational interviews is when you get to know hiring managers and get into their good graces by asking for an informational interview and then apply for the job right away. This is similar to meeting with a person under false pretenses. It is possible that you will kill your chances for getting the job if the hiring managers feel that you were dishonest about your intentions. If you ask for an informational interview in connection with a job opening, you will likely hear that you should submit your resume or application in order to be considered.

Action point:
- Schedule informational interviews when networking and building relationships. They should be a part of your proactive career-development strategy.

25
You Are Really Prejudiced against Me!

~

During the interviewing process, interviewers will assess whether you are a good fit for the job and whether your experiences are the right match. That is their job. Your job is to patiently and logically walk them through how and why you will succeed in the role.

You should not blame the interviewing team for something they are doing or not doing. However, if you feel that you have been wronged when applying, you may want to talk to an attorney, as opposed to rehashing it with the hiring team.

I met for an informational interview with a young man at the behest of someone in my network. He was interested in a career as a credit analyst. Yet all of his prior experiences, future goals, and interests were pointing at the track of a financial analyst in the investment management field. When I questioned whether the credit analyst's path was what he really wanted, he kept insisting that he would be very interested in being on my team. At that time he had already broken the rule of getting into an informational interview under false pretenses, while he actually wanted to apply. When I persisted in evaluating what his true career goals were, he got visibly upset and interrupted the meeting, declaring that I was clearly prejudiced against him.

My immediate next step was to talk to the contact who had provided the introduction. He was appalled by this behavior, apologized profusely, and assured me that he would never refer this individual to anyone. As you might guess, my team did not consider this person for the vacancy.

26
I Don't Really Care about the Prescreen

Prescreens are a very common way to make a first – typically phone or video conferencing – contact with an applicant. Prescreeners have several goals, including determining if you meet the eligibility requirements beyond what's on your resume. They also investigate your salary expectations and why you want to apply. The lesser-known purpose of prescreens is to check your verbal communication skills and how you interact on the phone. In an age when communication skills are rapidly deteriorating, it is a good way to screen out applicants.

Prescreens are akin to speed dating and can be as quick as five to fifteen minutes. Your screener, typically a member of the recruiting team and not a subject-matter expert in the job, will verify and ascertain data facts.

One of key goals of prescreens is to identify viable candidates and reduce time wasted on interviews. Consequently, you must put a 150 percent effort into prescreens. You must be very prepared and focused during this stage. The biggest mistake people make, one that knocks them out of the running, is when they assume that their credentials will carry them to the interviews. Another very common error is not having enough respect for the members of the recruiting team who conduct prescreens. This is a big, applicant-eliminating error.

Action point:
- Prepare for a prescreen to be a sprint. Do not usurp the time allotted and focus on being to-the-point, succinct, and focused.

27
Clothes, Shoes, and Hairdos

~

There is an old Russian saying: *Po odezke vstrechayut, po umu provazhayut.* It means that one is greeted by her or his dress and is seen off by her or his mind. Another way to say it is that one's dress gives others an initial impression, and one's mind leaves the lasting impression. We may argue endlessly whether it is right or wrong to pay attention to form over substance (or clothes over experience and talents) as the first impression. What's important is to recognize that it's a fact and to understand what you need to do to manage perceptions.

Your goal is to make a strong first impression or, at a minimum, ensure that the first impression does not knock you out of the running. Dressing well and dressing for the occasion is a valuable skill to have. It has little to do with your level of income. It is true that earlier in our careers budgets are tight. Moreover, research shows that younger generations now are poorer than their parents were, and they also have more debt. Yet this is one skill (both the clothes and the attitude toward your appearance) that will keep repaying you.

"I'll wear what I want when I want!" – This declaration does not work when it comes to interviewing. While you may want to find out what the expectations are for dressing for an interview, the majority of industries and companies expect you to be dressed in a suit (and a tie for men). Take pride in your appearance! It tells interviewers that you are attentive, detail-oriented, well-informed, and professional. Anybody can dress down for a wrinkled pajama party. Try dressing up!

Cleanliness is everything, especially with lighter clothes. Otherwise, you signal to your interviewer that you do not care. Prospective employers do not need people who do not care. Similarly, there is nothing worse than dirty, wrinkled, or unironed clothes at an interview. What your prospective employers may think about is: *Could this person not take the time to prepare? Did she or he not bother showering? Does this individual not really want the job?* While we do not have a culture of ironing clothes in the US anymore, and we would rather pull clothes out of the dryer and let them straighten on their own, I encourage you to invest in an iron and a good ironing board. Learn how to press clothes. Chances are that your parents and grandparents know how to do it, and they will be happy to teach you. This skill will last you a lifetime.

Shoes are an inseparable part of our image, and many people miss the mark. If you decide to show up for an interview in flip-flops, sandals, sport shoes, or hiking footwear, you may just as well skip the interview altogether. You do not have to have brand-new shoes. What's important is to have cleaned and well-polished shoes, which will require a sense of care, time to prepare, and a focus on small details. Some no-no's are white socks with black shoes, patterned socks or socks that are slightly different shades, or flashy socks that will distract your interviewers when you walk around.

Last but not least, a well-groomed candidate will have a clean shave (for men), a nice haircut, and clean, trimmed nails. Whatever you do, your appearance should not distract interviewers from who you are as a candidate. Anything off the norm will stick out like a sore thumb and will send your prospective employers messages contrary to what you are working so hard to achieve during your interviews: showing them that you are the best person for the job!

Action points:
- Create a personal checklist that includes clothing, appearance, footwear, and other physical attributes of your image. Include specific descriptions for each.
- Determine what the appearance expectations are for the subject industry, company, and interviewers.

28
I Am so Awesome for this Job!!!

~

Employers value confidence and drive in candidates. At times these qualities can border on cockiness. Yet there is hardly anyone who appreciates boasting, overconfidence, and meritless applicants using lots of clichés on their cover letters and other written communications.

What employers want to see is confidence that you are the best employee possible for the job – confidence rooted in your skills and knowledge. What they do not want to hear is you dropping words such as *great, excellent, best choice,* and other clichés about your candidacy. When you do, you risk awakening the doze-off-and-move-on virus.

Words are cheap, and track record is everything. This is much more challenging for applicants with little to no work experience. In those instances, experiences outside your line of business matter. I am referring to your transferable skills. Let your prospective team members establish that you are the best candidate based on what you have accomplished and from qualities that you may possess.

This is where preparation and taking ample time to draft your communications make a world of difference. Balance discussing your strengths with what is important for your future employers, including why you want the job, what value you will create, and how you qualify.

Action points:
- Work to eliminate clichés in reference to yourself in written and verbal speech.
- Practice talking in front of others about what you bring to the table and why you are the right choice.

29
I Have no Idea What I Am Applying For

~

More often than you might think, individuals apply for jobs that they do not know much about, beyond what is written in job descriptions. While potential employers may not expect you to know every little detail, they still expect that you will be familiar with the industry, their company, and the job proper. If you are not, you have not done your due diligence, and this will lower your chances to get the job.

Using an example from my industry, commercial banking, we frequently interview candidates new to the role of credit analysts. Sometimes applicants confuse us with wealth or investment management, investment banking, or something else that has nothing to do with the job of a credit analyst in our space. That's when you want to get on to the next interviewee, unless you are so desperate for candidates that you might want to give someone a chance.

There is ample information about positions and companies to be gained through general Internet research or through your networks. Make sure that you know your data well enough not to confuse it with something else during the interview. Last but not least, be cautious about switching midway and claiming that that particular job is what you want to do, once you learn what it entails (more on this later in the book). Adaptability does not exonerate you from being unprepared. You signal to the interviewer that you'd apply for anything, and that is not a flattering quality.

Action point:
- Truly understand what the job, company, and industry entail. If you are not clear, be sure to do your due diligence before applying.

30
Do Your Homework!

~

It is critical for you as a job hunter to do your homework about prospective employers and their industries to demonstrate that you know they are quality material. This also helps ensure that you make an educated career decision. Unprepared candidates are one of recruiters' and hiring managers' greatest pet peeves! They do not appreciate people wasting their time.

Your industry research should include the following: what the industry does, its key players, key products and services offered, and industry trends and outlook. Company research should include: knowledge of what it does, its clients' profiles, its primary differentiators and competitive qualities, key products or services, main competitors, key news, trends and outlook, financial condition (if available), and in some instances, familiarity with key executives' profiles.

As you are applying for a specific job, you must demonstrate a good understanding of what it entails. You may not always know all the intricate details, but you should have an understanding of the main responsibilities, how it fits into the company's structure, and what experiences are required and desired. More specific questions can be answered during the interview, but you have to know the essentials to help separate you from other contenders.

Action points:
- Create a checklist of what you need to learn about the company, its market, and its industry.
- Make a list of questions that you'd like to have answered during the interview. As a bonus, see the example of a brief industry analysis summary of commercial banking, found at the back of this book.

31
I Didn't Really Think You'd Check

~

If you think that your prospective employers will not verify your educational degrees, GPA, licenses, past places of employment, the fact that you left prior companies in a good standing, your prior salary or title, and other verbal or written claims you make, you may be in for a rude awakening. In all honesty, some employers may not check because they may not have the resources and experience. In other instances, HR staffers may be apprehensive about inquiries out of fear of legal liability. Nevertheless, do you want to make a bet that your prospective employer is that company?

The best philosophy you should live by is to be honest. It just so happens that sooner or later dishonest people get caught, and that can cost them their careers. Before you decide to provide false information, think about the risk you would be taking. There are ample examples of individuals deliberately misleading their employers and their contacts, ultimately to the detriment of everything they worked so hard to build.

By way of example, here is a word of caution about being "selective" with facts: some might consider inputting their major GPA because it is higher than their total GPA and meets the minimum threshold to apply for a job. Others might say that they managed a large team, while most employees were only dotted-line reporting to them. When dealing with a gray area, be careful about how what you say could be interpreted when the true information comes out.

Action points:
- Interview and network honestly.
- Fact check information you provide to make sure that there are no deliberate or unintended misrepresentations.

32
What Happens Online, Stays Online

The Internet is a feat of technology, but it can be ruinous to a career because what happens online stays online. Many of us have done something that we might not want out there, years from today. It is similar to an unsightly tattoo that was a spur-of-the-moment decision, but is now an ugly reminder of an unwise impulse. Even if there are techniques or services to clean up your Internet footprint, the jury is still out on whether they are foolproof. Assume that everything is permanent.

Suppose that you are the captain of a team, and in the heat of a game you offer a few "inspirational" words. Among these words are: "They will scream like little girls when we are done with them." Imagine that a video of it is posted on YouTube, and your prospective hiring manager views it. What if the interviewer is a woman, a father who has a daughter, or just a modern person devoid of the sexism that was more prevalent in the past? While you may not be a sexist, people might interpret your remarks as immature or as a hint of future behavior that would be unacceptable in a professional setting.

We typically get one chance to impress interviewers, and you may have just blown yours. Fair or not, in a competitive labor environment, that's all it takes. People move on to the next candidate. The selection process is not about second chances.

Action points:
- Always think before you do something and about longer-term implications (think of past examples of people whose racism was revealed to the public, and how their actions were documented for their descendants to be ashamed of).
- Work to keep your electronic footprint as clean and as reputable as possible.

33
What's with the Formalities?

~

We have become casual and informal in our behavior, clothing, and communication, especially in the United States. Some may say that we are too casual. This does not mean that the interview process will be informal. It still retains elements of a formal ritual of courtship. To be successful in interviewing, it is critical to know the expectations and the range of acceptable behaviors within your industry. You should also err on the side of caution and conservatism.

The above by no means should be interpreted as advising you against having your own style and personality. It is about having the maturity to do what is appropriate and having a healthy respect for structure and for following the rules. For instance, if you need to wear a suit and tie (for men), do not show up in khakis – or worse yet, jeans – just to demonstrate that you are clueless or rebellious.

Other formal elements of the interview include being proper and professional in your written communication. This includes addressing people as Mr. or Ms., thanking them for their consideration, and not using casual phrases such as "hey" and "what's going on." Similarly, face-to-face interaction includes knowing not to speak out of turn, saying what's appropriate, not being argumentative, and addressing more senior people as "Ms. Smith" or "Mr. Jones", until you are given permission to use their first names.

Action points:
- Find out what the expected behaviors are in your industry.
- Make a list of formal behaviors attributed to interviews and practice them. See an example of one industry at the end of this book.

34
Organizing Your Portfolio

When you are gearing up for interviews, it is a good idea to buy and have ready to go various "supplies" that will accompany you for your interviews. It is also good to create a checklist for various other items that will ensure a successful application cycle. Below are the most essential items, but the list is not all-inclusive.

Must-haves:
- Notepad(s) and pens
- Business cards
- Extra copies of your resume (and before that, resume paper, if you prefer a particular paper style and quality)
- Interview agenda, address, directions, and anything else to help you get to and from the interview and have flawless meetings

- A list of questions for your prospective employer and notes from your research
- Breath fresheners or mints to ensure that your breath does not kill your chances to get the job
- A portfolio to carry and organize all your accessories in

Other items to consider:
- Car charger or an extra battery for your (smart) phone to ensure that it will function when you need it
- Calendar in your smart phone or paper calendar, if you are old-school
- Tissues, especially if you are not feeling well
- Lip balm, if you are in parts of the world where cold or windy weather conditions result in cracked lips
- Hand cream, if your hands have unsightly dryness

35
The Power of Practice

~

Interviewing is something most people are not good at because they do not do it enough. Practice is essential for a variety of reasons. The most basic of those reasons is to give you personal confidence to present yourself in the best possible light. When you are not comfortable and confident while communicating with the interviewers, your mind is preoccupied by many thoughts and fears that compete for your attention. As a result, you can't showcase your true, best self.

Part of delivering top performance during your interviews is being comfortable with your voice, controlling its tone and inflection, breathing, and channeling your energy into being relaxed and confident. Below are three steps that can help.

Step 1: Practice out loud, hearing your voice, learning to talk smoothly (without gasping for air), being less tense, and answering questions concisely and energetically.

Step 2: Practice in front of a mirror to learn to understand and better manage your facial expressions, posture, and gestures.

Step 3: Ask someone to act as an interviewer, followed by an honest feedback session. There is a benefit to asking a less familiar person to provide you with feedback. People we know well can be hesitant to be honest with negative feedback.

Practice runs also help you build endurance. Just like sports, interviews can drain your physical and emotional energy. You do not want to be a player who runs out of steam after a few innings.

Action point:
- Make a list of two or three key strengths to continue building on and two or three key weaknesses whose negative impact you can reduce before you start interviewing.

36
Your Family May Be Doing You a Disservice

~

Your family and friends can be instrumental in helping open doors that will either be closed or that will take a while to get through. What is important is their ability to step out of your way when their job is done to help you do your job in networking, interviewing, and securing employment.

Why is this important? After a proper introduction is made, employers want to see independent people who are able to think and act on their own, regardless of their age. If you can't or if you are not given an opportunity to do so, your prospective employers may conclude that this is how you will behave in the workplace: lacking confidence, initiative, and the ability to get the job done without constant supervision.

Therefore, once you have been linked with a person or company you are interested in, ask your family members to step back. It is beneficial to have a conversation for a joint understanding of what their role will be even before you receive assistance. This also means that you need to be very grateful and respectful to those who assist you. Patience is another trait that may be required in working with your family as not all family members will step away easily. Work to prevent awkward and unacceptable moments, such as family members calling on your behalf to inquire about the status of your application, to negotiate your salary, or to vouch for you.

Action points:

- Establish mutual understanding of the help you need and when you will proceed on your own.
- When problems arise, address them respectfully, patiently, and with the personal touch that family and friends deserve.

37
Graceful Pullout

~

Regardless of your job-hunting strategy, it is important to be aware that the business world is a small world. Withdrawing from an application process is a very delicate matter that requires a strategy and tactful communication. The worst you can do is to go into hiding out of fear of appearing inappropriate or because you do not know what to do.

If you need to stop your application process, you should do it in a timely manner so that people do not waste their valuable resources considering you. Realize that one day you may be applying with the same individuals again. It won't help to build your personal reputation and brand if your interviewers toss you out of the running just because you failed to communicate properly a long time ago.

You will also need a reasonable explanation. Should you decide to have a cover story, make sure that the truth does not come out. Contact all the key players that you have been involved with so far, especially the key decision makers. Thank them for their time and explain why you will be unable to continue. A terrible example of not dealing with an ongoing application is a young man who did not show up for his scheduled interviews. When a team member called him, the applicant apologized and explained that he meant to call but did not have a chance to. He had already gotten a job. Do you think the hiring team will remember him? Count on it!

Action points:
- If you are withdrawing, consider having a conversation and giving the company a chance to respond.
- Make a list of people you need to contact and then think of the message and the best way to deliver it. Follow through!

38
I Am Looking for a Perfect Job

~

Does a perfect job or a perfect career really exist? (It is more likely to be a perfect career as opposed to just a job.) Maybe it does. If you are one of the lucky people who finds one, hold on to it with everything you've got. For the rest of us, finding that ultimate career path is a matter of trial and error. This process can take time – sometimes, quite a bit of time.

What you may want to ask yourself is how you would describe that perfect job. Is it a desire to make a difference in the world or your community, to utilize certain skills, to make money, to serve as means to another end, or something else? Without asking these questions, it is very difficult to have a strategy and a direction to reach the goal of a perfect career. Identify the most important elements as opposed to everything under the sun.

Part of your search will be finding the right industry, company, non-profit organization, a line of business, or a function that gives you the greatest satisfaction. You should consider building transferable skills as part of this journey. They will allow you to be marketable and change direction if you need to.

You may experience unexpected twists that can take you in a somewhat different direction than you planned; it might not be something you'd wanted to do at the time. Consider taking a chance for a period of time because chances can lead to something good that you did not expect.

Finally, the search for a perfect career is not only about the finish line but also about the journey to discover who you are and what matters the most to you. Experiences along the way, even if unrelated on the surface, will likely be just as valuable in getting you to that "perfect" place.

39
Making Your
Communications Matter

Based on articles in the general press, research, and the common knowledge of hiring teams, writing skills are rapidly disappearing in the corporate world. Yet strong business writing skills are an essential quality of any successful candidate. In addition to a strong knowledge of grammar, syntax, punctuation, and other elements, you have to learn to write succinctly and with purpose.

Identify one or two key reasons and messages you'd like to communicate to your readers in your cover letters, e-mails, thank-you letters, and other correspondence. If any content does not support the intent of your writing, strike it mercilessly. For example, if you are writing a cover letter, what is its purpose? If you are trying to communicate how your background matches the needs of a prospective employer *and* why you will be a successful hire, make sure that you are focused on that and only that. Always ask yourself: Why am I writing this?

Keep all your communications concise. Start with writing a bare minimum. You can always layer in more details, but it is much harder to cut than to add. Here is one example structure for an e-mail, inspired by the work of Andy Bounds, a communications expert from the United Kingdom: greeting, context for why you are writing, benefits to the person you are writing, your request (the ask) and timeline, if any, wrap-up and signature. Before sending, do not forget to proofread several times.

Although it is important to know the etiquette of written communication in your industry, also stay personable and true to your own style. Yes, you will need to learn to write in your own style as opposed to replicating the template language provided in books on how to write cover letters.

DURING THE INTERVIEW

40
I'll Be There as Soon as I Can

~~

When it comes to interviews (and not just interviews), punctuality is everything. If you are not early, you are late! You should arrive at least ten to fifteen minutes earlier than required and announce your arrival. Also, build in extra time to deal with the building security and to get to the floor where your interview will take place. If you have been told that you need to complete paperwork, consider coming thirty minutes ahead of time or even earlier.

While you should always be on time, it may happen that you run late. Firstly, minimize those instances. Secondly, communicate ahead of time that you may be late. Never call a couple of minutes before your scheduled time. There is not enough time to rearrange the day, especially when multiple interviews are scheduled. Try calling first; building a personal connection is the key task of a job seeker. If you are driving and need to call or send a message, pull over safely. You do not want to hurt yourself or another person while trying to get a job. Saving a few minutes is not worth it. Thirdly, do not forget that an apology goes a long way – something people forget. Lastly, always remain composed and never freak out when letting the interviewer know that you will be late.

What hiring managers never want to hear is that you will be there "as soon as you can." It is your responsibility to get to an interview on time! Barring accidents and events truly outside of your control, running late tells prospective employers that you can't manage your time, are not organized, do not want the job enough, or simply may not deserve it.

Action points:
- Map the interview route in order to arrive ahead of time.
- Have all contact details within reach, in case you are late.

41
Dry Run

~

Just as you should practice for your interviews, it could be beneficial to do a dry run to get to the location, if you are in the area. It can help reduce the stress of travel to interviews in an unfamiliar area and help you focus on the interview proper. On the negative side, extra travel can have negative environmental impact that more and more people are conscious about and strive to reduce.

The dry-run strategy can be particularly valuable in places like Boston. If you have ever been to our fabulous city, you know well that street signs are often missing or hard to find, roads are narrow and often one-way, and construction never seems to ends. It is very easy to take a wrong turn, from which it may be impossible to recover for a while. This is especially true in the Financial District. One wrong move and you are outside the area. It may take another 10-15 minutes to make your way back, if you are lucky. Throw in regular and absolutely unpredictable construction work that blocks that one and only one-way road, and eve the luck of the Irish will not save you.

If you have prior interviewing experience, you know that at times everything that can go wrong, does go wrong. Traffic comes to a standstill, buses run late, trains break down, and flight connections get missed. Other common examples are going to the wrong building, a wrong entrance, overshooting the address where you need to be, being pulled over by a cop because you are driving in less than a focused way, needing to look for parking, and elevators being out of order.

Leave ample time to get to the interview, which may require clearing a good portion of your day, or even the entire day. Interviewers are less likely to be accommodating and forgiving with junior applicants, as competition for those jobs tends to be even greater because more people are after them.

42

I Need a Job, Not a Lesson on Your Company.

~

For prospective employers, the game of interviewing can be as nerve-racking as it is for you, the interviewee. It combines the excitement of discovering what the candidate is all about, the fear of making a wrong and costly decision, the pain of even needing to be in the market for a new hire when they would rather get their actual work done, and the goal of finding the best person possible that their budget can afford. Think about this as you are preparing for an interview. If you want a job but don't care to learn about your prospective employer, hiring teams do not want you.

Every employer tends to believe that their company is a special place to work and better than anything out there. Interviewers expect you to share at least some of the same enthusiasm. While you can learn a great deal from information available on the Internet and through your networks, there is no better way to understand the company and the team than by asking people who do the actual work.

Prepare questions that will help you understand the culture of your prospective employer, its structure, its atmosphere, goals, direction, and the strategy to get there. Similarly, learn about the team that you are applying for: its dynamics, values, and the qualities expected in a new recruit. Do not forget to understand the team leader and her or his priorities.

Some individuals believe that if given a choice between an outstanding company and a dysfunctional team or a dysfunctional company and an outstanding team, they would choose the latter. I tend to agree. The interview is possibly your only opportunity to truly figure out your prospective employer.

43
I Finally Get It!

~

Few companies are good at expressing what a job truly entails in job descriptions. If you have read as many job descriptions as some of us have over the years, you will conclude that most employers are looking for a superwoman or a superman. It is remarkable how all-encompassing some job descriptions are. You might get the sense that there is not enough time in the day to do everything outlined. Do not let such job descriptions discourage you!

You are expected to have some baseline under-standing of what the job is all about, whether from prior experiences or through your independent research. Make sure that you develop several questions that will allow you to understand what the job will require – questions that are insightful and not superficial. There is nothing sadder than an interviewee who asks boring questions that can be easily answered by doing basic research, who uses clichéd questions that everybody else asks, or who has no questions at all.

Remember that you will have a chance to ask only a few questions, so you need to pick quickly and effectively what questions on your list are the most relevant.

Action points:
- If your prior experiences and skills do not match what's in the job description, prepare to justify why you are the right candidate for the job.
- If information about the job indicates a major disconnect with your true interests, assess whether it is time to pull out of the running.

44

Interviews Are Not Just about Eye Contact

~

Eye contact is an essential part of creating a personal presence during your interview. It is one of the elements that you will be evaluated on. While acceptable norms of eye contact can vary widely across the globe from culture to culture, in the United States and some other countries it is similar to a good handshake. It can tell the person you are meeting with a lot about your background, maturity, self-confidence, and ability to interact comfortably with others.

I recall interviewing a young woman who, without a doubt, exuded a strong sense of confidence without overdoing it. She was confident, composed beyond her years, relaxed, and comfortable. In addition to her experiences and aptitude, how she carried herself and maintained eye contact "told" interviewers that she had the ability to work with, learn from, and hold her ground with demanding and experienced commercial bankers without being intimidated by them.

How to "do" eye contact correctly is often misunderstood, and it is quite often overdone. Maintaining eye contact does not mean staring at the interviewer and watching her or his every word and move without blinking one's eyes. That can be very uncomfortable and off-putting. You are not there to hypnotize or intimidate people. You are not there to charm your interviewers either – well, perhaps a bit, but not with your looks and your beautiful eyes but with your intelligence.

Action points:
- Practice eye contact with an interviewing partner to develop a fine balance of focusing without staring.
- Ask others to observe and provide feedback on your eye contact and posture.

45

Your Attention Just Wandered Off

~

Every interviewee is faced with numerous distractions. They range from seeing people passing by when you are facing a glassed-in hallway, to the noise of emergency vehicles, construction work, and people popping in and out of the interview room. You must learn to maintain a high degree of focus on the interviewer and on your performance. The hiring team will draw conclusions about your ability to stay focused on business goals from how focused you are during the interview.

If you shift your attention to another person outside the conference room, react to a slight noise, or lose your train of thought, interviewers can conclude that you may not be interested in the job or that this is how you will perform in the role. If your eyes are focused on something other than the interviewer, it is disrespectful and helps her or him to conclude that the job is not for you.

An extreme example of an unfocused job seeker is a person who kept staring at a young woman whose desk was behind the glass wall he was facing. The staring was so obvious and made the woman so uncomfortable that she spoke with the hiring manager right after the interview. He never got the job. Remember that part of your presence is actually to be present and not focused on anything else.

Action points:
- If you have a tendency to be easily distracted, practice more than an average person, including with various distractions deliberately interrupting your concentration.
- Without staring, make sure that the interviewer is your primary focus; this is the key to interviewing successfully.

46
Why Your Posture Matters

Many of us remember our parents constantly nagging us: Straighten your back. Don't slouch. Keep your head up straight. These reminders were constant and quite annoying at the time. First and foremost, the reminders had to do with having a healthy posture and a straight back. Fast forward to today. The unexpected benefit of those reminders is how we carry ourselves in our daily lives, including during interviews.

You may have known or seen individuals whose presence filled an entire room. You may have heard these phrases: "bigger than life" or "confident in her skin." People with these qualities do not need to be loud, obnoxious, or famous. Their presence is about how they carry themselves, how they speak, the clothes they wear, and how they interact with other people. An important element of their presence is their body language. It speaks volumes to their prospective employer at interviews. Everything starts with posture.

Interviewers have a very limited amount of time to discover and understand your technical skills, your aptitude, your capabilities, your talents, and the likelihood that you will become a well-performing employee. As a result, they are like hawks, watching for clues and details, with body language being one of those tremendous giveaways.

Action point:
- Practice, practice, and practice. Assume a straight posture, whether you are standing or sitting. Loosen up and relax your shoulders. Straighten your head so that it is not inclined up or down too much. Keep your hands in front of you when sitting or comfortably to your sides when standing.

47

The Rooster Effect

~

Have you ever met people who exude an incredible amount of confidence and strength, without puffing up like birds of paradise? How about the opposite: individuals who stand with chin and chest forward, trying to create an appearance of the same, while everyone around them knows that they are faking it? They remind me a lot of roosters, and I call it the rooster effect.

This kind of behavior is particularly common among younger individuals. You can see them often in Boston's Financial District or around Wall Street in New York. Their inexperience and lack of inner confidence shines through so they try to compensate in their external appearance with extra "puffiness." In many instances these shortfalls and lack of maturity can and will be cured after years of real life.

For experienced interviewers, this kind of behavior is less than appealing. Not only is it indicative of a lack of maturity, it is also off-putting to many prospective team members who have little tolerance for stand-offish colleagues. Even if this is not the intent and is instead an internal defense mechanism to build better confidence, it may prevent you from demonstrating the qualities that could qualify you for a particular job. You may get mistakenly (or not mistakenly) labeled as a weak team player, pompous, overconfident, arrogant, and not having good social skills. The best advice is to be yourself and develop confidence by being who you are.

Action points:
- Ask people who are likely to be honest with you about your appearance, your behavior, and how you come across visually.
- Be aware of your behavior and how you come across.

48
Hijacking the Interview

~

Whether it is a buyer's or a seller's job market, recruiting teams are in charge, and you are their guest – not the other way around. Some job seekers forget this and highjack the interview with their own questions. This happens for various reasons, including a desire to impress prospective employers, to assert themselves, to avoid answering questions, or because they are clueless about what's appropriate.

This does not mean that you can't ask questions, but you need to know when it is appropriate to do so. Most commonly, you will have an opportunity to ask questions toward the end of an interview. You also need to remember that you will likely have time for just two to three questions, and you need to make them count. You should have a list of questions prepared in advance. Yet you should adapt to the situation and only bring up questions that make the most sense in light of your conversation so far.

I would caution you against using your questions as a way to avoid answering someone else's or to distract the interviewer from her or his questioning strategy. The best approach is to be honest. If you do not have an answer or a satisfactory (in your opinion) answer, just say so or find the next closest example. An interviewer with even a bit of experience will keep bringing you back if you are not answering certain questions. It means that the interviewer finds them relevant. Even if it is not your intent, be aware of how your behavior may be interpreted.

Action points:
- If you like to chat, keep reminding yourself that you are a guest at an interview.
- If you find that the interviewer is talking a lot, you need to turn the tables because you are there to "sell" yourself.

49

Just Answer the Question!

~

One of the most frustrating moments for a hiring professional during an interview is when questions are not being answered. You have a very limited amount of time to get to know a candidate, and it's frustrating when she or he, for whatever reason, does not give you a straight answer. At that moment you do not really care whether it is an inexperienced person who is simply not able to offer an example to answer your question or if it is a person who has something to hide. The bottom line is that the person is wasting your valuable time!

If an interviewer senses that you may just need "help" with getting back to the question that's being asked, she or he may decide to give you one or two more chances. This typically happens when interviewers ask so-called behavioral questions. She or he wants to understand how you reacted or are likely to react to specific circumstances. If you feel that the person on the opposite side of the table brings you back more than once, be aware that you may not be answering the questions and may need to focus. You may be at a point where you are not creating the most favorable impression.

It may happen from time to time that you don't have an example to offer regarding a particular behavior. Yet in many instances, you may have done something similar enough that it can be used as an adequate illustration.

Action points:
- Resist answering questions in a way that you feel the interviewer may prefer for you to answer them.
- Remember to never BS your interviewers as truth has a tendency to come out.
- Help the interviewer learn about the real you and what value and qualities you bring to the table.

50
I Thought We Had Thirty More Minutes

~

Face-to-face interviews typically last thirty to sixty minutes, with the hiring manager likely spending a longer time with a candidate because she or he stands to benefit the most from a new hire. Some interviews, though, can be much shorter than otherwise scheduled and expected. This is likely not good news, unless a prospective employer likes you so much that she or he considers extending an offer to you. Much shorter interviews tend to indicate that your interview did not go well.

There are various reasons why interviews get cut short, but most can be grouped as follows: the candidate is too nervous, does not have decent social skills, is not answering questions, is being elusive, seems to be disinterested, or is just not the right fit. To the credit of some interviewers, they may be merciful toward inexperienced applicants by completing the interview so as not to crush their tiny, emergent egos. As for the rest, a quick and easy interview is likely bad news.

Fortunately, if you have a sense of self-awareness and can read interviewers' signals, you will be able to notice that something is wrong. First, do not panic – breathe! Second, do your best to answer the questions that are being posed to you. Third, tell your prospective employer why you are a strong – if not the best – candidate. Leave clichés and empty phrases behind and talk to the interviewer. Last, interviews typically include meetings with more than one person, and you may get a chance to do damage control with the interviewers who follow.

Action points:
- Through mock interviews, you should be able to catch the fact that your interviewing skills are inadequate.
- If your interviews are quick and short without a job offer, this is a signal that you have a problem to address.

51
Interviewers Are Not Your Friends!

~

Some interviewers are very professional and kind people. Their nature is to make prospective job seekers comfortable and relaxed. It does not mean that they are your friends, want to be your friends, or are there to make you feel good about yourself. Do not mistake a pleasant, friendly demeanor for an invitation to become friends.

One of the benefits for any interviewer of making you feel very comfortable and relaxed is to get to know the real you. A number of interviewees will be guarded and put on a performance as a result of "training" received from information available online, through career offices, books, and other sources. Some will be nervous and uncomfortable about projecting who they really are. Instead, they portray someone they think they should be or who they think interviewers want to see. Thus, an experienced interviewer has to pull you out of that shell to see what you are all about. Without that, they risk getting an individual who might not work out for the job.

If you encounter a friendly and comfortable environment during an interview, do not forget that you are a guest who is expected to be on her or his best behavior. A friend of mine recounted a story of an interviewee who relaxed so much that when he heard a birthday celebration in an adjacent office, he asked if he could have a slice of cake. You can guess the outcome of that interview. No matter how personable the interviewers are, do not forget proper norms of behavior.

Action point:
- If you have trouble intuiting what kind of behavior is expected, at least remember to never deviate from what is proper and highly respectable. Err on the side of caution.

52
What Are Your Hours?

~

If you are a salaried employee working in the United States, you probably know that the so-called forty-hour week is not a forty-hour week any more. There is plenty of research on this subject, and it is a well-established fact in many industries and companies. When it comes to salaried employees or even those on hourly pay, nobody wants employees who can't wait to clock out.

Employers want engaged employees who are not dying to see their day (or night) end. Many employers will say that they need employees who'd do whatever it takes to get the job done. That means being driven and committed, flexible when needed, and willing to work longer hours and, more importantly, to work them productively and effectively. It does not mean working 24-7, although some companies have that kind of corporate culture. Thus, make sure that you do your homework. If the culture and expectations are not for you, why even apply? And if you know what they are, does it really make sense to ask, if you risk being ruled out from the running?

There are, however, indirect ways to find out what the expectations are and to communicate your needs or preferences. Ask interviewers who do the actual work to walk through their typical day. Listen between the lines when the hiring manager talks about attendance, flexibility, and expectations. Ask someone you know well and trust about the company. This is your behind-the-scenes research. Some interviews may include shadowing, which is a great way to see the work being done. For more junior candidates, internships are a great way to look inside and have essentially an on-the-job, continuous interview. Lastly, if you have particular family work-life balance needs, you need to find a way to communicate them delicately yet honestly.

53
When May I Take My Sabbatical?

~

When you earn it! That's the most direct and professional answer you will likely receive, although there's a good probability you will be knocked out of the running. You have not even started working for the employer, and you are already thinking about venturing off to do something else. While it might involve great and necessary work, it will take you away from your employer for an extended period of time, often with full pay. What's in it for your employer? If the competition for a position is high, this is one of those candidacy-torpedoing questions you should not be asking.

If you do, it is certainly to the benefit of your interviewers because it gives them a chance to weed out those who do not belong. In a way, prospective employers are grateful when they are able to get a glimpse of what's truly on the interviewees' minds. In the game of finding the right match for both sides, employers often need to draw conclusions from your responses as well as your questions to establish who the persons in front of them is.

What this means is that you should remember two things: a) understand what is appropriate and what is not appropriate to ask (a sabbatical question being one of them), and b) keep your mouth shut about certain things and adjust your expectations to keep your job in the long run. This does not mean that you should be dishonest. What it means is that you should postpone some goals – like a sabbatical – until the time is right.

Action point:

- If you do not know what is appropriate to ask, make a list and practice "controlling" your questions and taming behaviors that are not appropriate.

54
Interacting with Other Candidates

~

Observing how candidates interact with their competition is an even better way to assess prospective applicants than how they interact with staff members, such as recruiters and receptionists. Expect to be watched and to have your reactions observed, recorded, and judged.

It is potentially a tense situation knowing that any one of the other applicants could snatch your job away. Some applicants do not open up at all, and sit in isolation. Some can be standoffish, adversarial, and even confrontational. Still others put on a superficially friendly face that's fake and disingenuous. Only a few interviewees are genuinely friendly and can interact comfortably with others.

Prospective employers will be thinking about many questions while watching your interaction with competition: Do you have the professionalism to handle this situation with grace and the spirit of good sportsmanship? How comfortable are you with starting a conversation and finding common ground, without being too invasive and imposing with your presence? Can you hold your ground in a situation where you know nothing about these individuals? Do you seem to be in your element? What social skills do you exhibit in these exchanges?

It is always great to see candidates who maintain eye contact, who engage others in conversations when appropriate, who are able to find a common theme for a brief discussion, and who can be friendly, natural, and engaging.

Action point:
- With fellow applicants, act in a manner that would mean they'd enjoy working with you if both of you were to be hired. That's the best tribute to your interpersonal skills.

55
Is It Hot in Here Or Is It Just Me?

~

Few of us are comfortable with interviewing because it is not something we do regularly. Yet, there are some who are paralyzed when facing prospective employers, to the point of failing the interview. If you feel very nervous during interviews – if you tend to freeze, sweat, or exhibit other physical or psychological reactions when facing a prospective employer – you have to deal with it sooner rather than later to give yourself a fighting chance. Avoidance is a terrible plan.

What you need is as much practice as possible. You can accomplish this by a variety of means, but the best practice is with people you do not know. Informational interviews are one such option. Another is to do full practice runs with someone who does not know you well so that there is no pressure to go easy on you. The goal is to put you through the full rigor of actual interviews.

A brutally honest feedback session is a bonus. Do everything possible to push yourself out of your comfort zone. If you choose not to, you risk not showing your real potential and failing to succeed. Interviews are somewhat similar to anecdotal knowledge about getting in to Harvard University – one of the hardest things is getting in, and you need to master this stage before you can move to the next.

Remember that the majority of interviewers will not bother making adjustments for your fears and discomforts in order to make you more comfortable. Why? They may perceive you to be a "project" even before you have the job, one who would require an extra effort to develop interpersonal skill in the future. People do not have time for projects!

Action point:
- The first step is recognizing that you have a problem with freezing during interviews. The next step is addressing it.

56
I Am Just Too Much Even for Me

~

Confident and driven candidates are what interviewers like to see. Yet it is important not to overdo your confidence. It can be quite uncomfortable and even disturbing for prospective employers to face a person who is too much even for herself or himself to handle. If your confidence shifts into the realm of being too intense and is displayed right in an interviewer's face, that can be very unsettling.

In this, as in some other situations provided thus far, the challenge is overcoming a lack of self-awareness. Interviewees are not aware of how they actually behave and how they are perceived. Their intentions may be in the right place, but it does not mean that they channel them appropriately.

Another problem is potentially overcompensating because in reality a candidate is not confident or comfortable. Many interviewers have faced candidates who stared intently into their eyes or who demonstrated such intense behaviors that the interviewers could not wait to get out of the conference room. Unless your goal is to try to intimidate or scare your interviewers, you may want to dial back and better channel your confidence and assertiveness.

Action points:
- As part of interview practice, ask others to evaluate how intense you appear in your eye contact, posture, speech, and gestures.
- If people tell you that you are too intense and need to adjust your approach, you should objectively evaluate their feedback and decide whether you need to soften your presentation.

57

I Am a Professional Interviewer

~

Some interviewees view themselves as professionals in the trade of interviewing because they have been interviewing often. A side effect of such "professionalism" is overconfidence and being unaware of very basic interviewing flaws. Another miscalculation is when so-called experienced interviewees attempt to manipulate their interviewers, forgetting about who runs the show.

There is a high probability that those who will interview you have materially more experience in dealing with applicants. If they catch even the slightest hint that you are attempting to control, influence, or in any way manipulate the interview, their reaction will be rather unpleasant for many reasons. It will range from feeling that you are wasting their time to indignation over the fact that someone has the audacity to manipulate the interview. Lastly, those who believe themselves to be the most experienced, in reality end up making the most elementary interviewing errors. This is caused by their overconfidence, even arrogance, and by not spending enough time to understand the interviewing essentials.

Action point:
- If you want to truly master interviews, your plan should include the following:
  - o Understand and work to meet all key expectations.
  - o Maintain a high level of self-awareness.
  - o Capitalize on your main strengths.
  - o Identify and reduce a couple of key weaknesses.
  - o Practice with ample and objective feedback.

58
Don't Act Like the Job Is Guaranteed

Whether you are an internal or external candidate, with or without connections, over- or under-qualified, go through the application process as if the job is not guaranteed and be eager to "fight" for every inch of ground to get it. Hiring managers do not like entitled people, even if they are the best choice their money can afford.

A good example is the story of an internal applicant who applied for a higher-level position within her team and presumed that she was the natural, well-qualified choice. Another candidate from a different division of the same company concluded no such thing. She went through the interview process with 150 percent effort and a genuine interest in the opportunity. While the latter candidate had similar credentials, how she acted impressed the hiring managers. They passed on the contender from their own team. They knew that they risked alienating that individual as a result of their decision, yet they opted in favor of an equally capable candidate without a sense of entitlement.

To help keep yourself in check, be as humble as possible. Even if you are someone's protégé, your supporters can carry you only so far. You need to do your part in earning the job. Do not assume anything – just focus on what's in front of you and make certain that you make your ride on the interviewing Ferris wheel as smooth as you can. Think of it this way: there are always people better than you, and you have to earn your place.

Action point:
- Even if you feel that you have an advantage over other interviewees, behave as if you are an underdog, without any bonus points that you can rely on.

59

Oh, That Was Quite a Sandwich!

~

Interviews are, to a great extent, about sharing. You want to share details of your background and accomplishments that can help support your credentials as the right candidate for the job. Some things, however, you do not want to share: one of them is your bad breath, whether it is due to issues with dental hygiene or to something as simple as a flavorful sandwich before the interview. Delicious foods that you enjoy before your interview can turn very quickly into your worst enemy and cost you the job.

It is remarkable how often this simple truth escapes people, and for many reasons. They range from being in a rush to get to the interview and forgetting a breath freshener to thinking that she or he will be okay, and the interviewer will not sense anything. Try envisioning a small conference room, and someone sitting just across the table from you. Any smells travel and spread very quickly. Your interviewers are bound to experience your odor, regardless of how bad or good it may be.

While some interviewers may have greater tolerance for unpleasant smells, they are certainly impacted by them. If the interview is not going well, your bad breath will exacerbate everything with a vengeance. Less than optimal conference room temperatures, dry air, or any other less than comfortable conditions will further escalate what's already unpleasant.

Action points:
- Get into the habit of becoming obsessed with using breath freshener before your interviews.
- Remember that interviewing is somewhat akin to sports competition: you need to accumulate the greatest number of points; every point matters; and bad breath takes those points away.

60
They Showed Us How to Do It in Training!

~

We have all been through school and on-the-job training programs. Although training can be a powerful tool in preparing us to do our job, nothing can replace on-the-job experience. In other words, theoretical experience is not experience quite yet.

It is likely that you will not have all relevant experience, especially if you are early in your career or are changing its direction. However, you may be able to demonstrate that some of your training can help you bridge the gap and be relevant to a future role. What's important is how you position your relevant training. This requires planning ahead of time and practicing delivering a balanced message.

Overzealous applicants try too hard to sell their prospective employers on hiring them. Their message is that they can do the job because they received certain training. People who say that they can do the job because they saw how to do it are naïve and cannot be taken seriously. What's important is to be honest about your lack of experience and focus on how prior training and other skills will help you be successful in a new role. Training without experience can be part of the overall picture but should not be your claim to competence.

Action points:
- If you know that you do not quite have the necessary relevant experience, identify training and experience that may be either transferable or that may provide a good foundation for being successful in bridging the gap.
- Plan your message about transferable experience or training without experience carefully. Your message needs to be honest, without exaggeration, logical, and confident.

61
Oh, That's What You Do?

~

"Oh, that's what you do?" Hiring managers sometimes witness this realization by applicants who have not done their homework about the job, the company, or the industry. This is certainly an awkward situation for both the interviewer and interviewee. "Okay, then I am ready to apply anyway," has been the reaction of some applicants, showing no hesitation to proceed with the interview process.

The fact that the job seeker did not know what she or he had been applying for can be the end of the process. It shows a lack of preparation, lack of attention to detail, and an immature attitude toward looking for employment. Granted, job descriptions can sometimes be unclear. So can the messages of recruiters in the first round of contact with applicants. Yet you should not use this as an excuse, or you should at least be extremely careful about the wording so that you do not come across as defensive or as pushing the blame onto others (especially if it is your failure). In the majority of cases though, it is the job seekers who fail to do their research. They apply without truly understanding what it is that they are making a bid for.

From the applicant's perspective, this is a tough situation to crawl out of. The most difficult situation is when you make this discovery during the actual interview. Whether you choose to pull out of interviews or continue, your strategy should be to preserve your dignity (and hopefully learn something from the snafu). Do not waste any more of the recruiting team's time. You will need to think quickly and most respectfully.

Action point:
- Always do your homework and know what it is you are applying for.

62

This Job is a Corolla, on My Way to a Lexus

~

A number of applicants see certain jobs as a way to get a foot in the door of a company or an industry. This is a common strategy. Where applicants go wrong is when they do not really want that first job and do not plan on staying in it for a period of time, even announcing that while interviewing. Their attitude is clear: they view the job as an entry-level "Corolla, before you can afford to buy a Lexus."

First and foremost, you should be concerned about building your reputation with the hiring team and the company and your overall reputation within the industry. That reputation should be built on honesty and not on promising something that you have no intention of fulfilling. Whatever promises you make, you should plan to honor them. Nobody likes to be a stepping stone, even when they are.

Second, while you may limit some information you channel to your prospective employers, you should never lie. For example, do not say that you are really interested in a job or a career track in the long term if it is not true. What you can focus on is what attracts you to this job (beyond the next step) and what value you can add to a prospective employer.

Last but not least, when you get the job, during your tenure gradually create a plan to move to the next opportunity. Then communicate it to your manager, secure her or his support, and work to implement it.

Action point:
- The key to a successful entry-level job is planning your message and fulfilling your commitment to the new employer.

63

How Quickly Can I Move to the Next Job?

~

Questions about how quickly you can move to the next job are typically a sure way to lose an opportunity. Companies hire employees to do the jobs at hand first and foremost, and then they worry about what these individuals can do next for the organization. In general, jobs without contracts require at least a one-year commitment before you can post for another opening within the same organization, but that may vary.

If you need to know how long you may have to be in a role before having an option to move on, you can reach out to your inside network. A roundabout way to inquire about time commitments is to ask about career tracks and your predecessors' development paths. If your interviewers do not volunteer this information during interviews, you may ask at the end of your meeting, when you know for certain that the company is interested in you and when you are likely to be extended an offer. Still, do not forget about the risks of bringing up this subject, and do it delicately.

A credit analyst who worked on my former team agreed to at least a two-year verbal commitment to the role (not a contract position) in return for a unique, extensive training and development opportunity. Instead, he left just shy of a year on the job. Although his performance was good, he failed to deliver on his promise. That team's members will think twice before hiring him in the future or before providing a reference.

Action points:
- Ensure that your interview strategy is focused on the job that you are interviewing for.
- Your verbal commitment to a job is just as important as a written one. It is an opportunity to establish or wreck your reputation in the industry.

64
Did I Tell You That My Mother Works Here?

~

Nepotism, cronyism, and other forms of favoring people because of an association to a particular group or individual are not uncommon in the corporate world. They range from very subtle and generally ethical acts of helping someone with an introduction to a prospective hiring manager (and nothing more) to exerting pressure to hire a candidate or instructing a hiring team to offer that person a job. Extreme examples can be viewed as unethical, an abuse of power, and even illegal.

If you have a connection that can facilitate your getting a job, beware! Hiring managers do not like the information that "your mother or father works here" flaunted in their faces. For hiring teams that look for the best quality candidates, they want employees who can stand on their own without the help of their relatives.

The disdain for behaviors that smack of nepotism becomes even more pronounced among those hiring managers who: a) advanced and grew on their own merits or b) have been negatively impacted by candidates who had an unfair advantage over them. In those instances, you may not get a fighting chance if you are someone's protégé. Be careful about how you take advantage of your connections so that they do not become a liability.

Action points:
- Monitor and manage your messages and how and when you make a reference to people who pull you through.
- Try to reduce or even eliminate references to your support group and focus on standing on your own merits. This will also help you to be respectful to those who have worked hard to advance on their own.

65
Name-Dropping Is
My Key Quality

~

One in every few applicants is a type well-known to hiring teams: the name-dropper. This person knows everybody. Everybody knows her or him. And everybody is her or his friend.

As you interview such a person, you can't help but ask yourself questions: Why are you mentioning all these names – is it to create a more favorable impression? If so, don't you have enough qualities to offer? Is it to show off or to impress me? Perhaps it is a pressure tactic to establish yourself as a VIP. Do not get me wrong – it is good to be connected. It is even better to be well-connected. However, as was noted in this book before, do not exaggerate or misrepresent facts.

There are so many ways that you may know people. You may know some people by having met them once or perhaps twice, but they have no idea who you are. Your contact may be an acquaintance who is vaguely familiar with you. Or, someone you know could be a good personal or professional friend who can provide you with good references. There are a few more shades of familiarity in between.

When sharing names of your connections during interviews, be specific about how you know them and in what capacity. Also, have a reason for citing your connections, or you will be branded as a name-dropper.

Action points:
- If there is no good reason for dropping names, keep them to yourself.
- Consider whether your contacts would approve of your dropping their names freely.

66

I Am a Team Player, Hard Worker, Go-Getter

~

Clichés are a thorn in the side of every recruiter and hiring manager because they do not say anything about a candidate (nothing good, that is). The most common clichés include, but are not limited to, the following: "I am team player." "Good communication is a key to every company's success." "I have strong writing skills." "I get the job done, no matter what."

Cover letters, resumes, and written and verbal messages are riddled with standard buzz phrases. Job seekers are falsely led to believe that it is what employers want to see and hear. What employers really want is behaviors, accomplishments, and a track record that speak to the same clichés without saying them. In other words, generic terms are a poor reflection on your candidacy. They do not say anything, and you are not sharing anything of value about yourself. Empty sentences frustrate interviewers and are fatal for your candidacy.

Instead, focus on providing examples that would offer colorful details about what, how, and why you did something as opposed to question avoidance and boring generic phrases. For example, evidence of being a strong team player is your ability to support a team of relationship managers, being proactive in reaching out to them, and consistently delivering on deadlines. Outstanding references that those relationship managers can provide on your behalf will help seal the deal.

Action points:
- Learn to identify empty buzz words and eradicate them from your vocabulary.
- Practice being able to provide examples that represent your greatest accomplishments in the areas of team work, problem solving, leadership, and others.

67

Oh, I Am a Complete Package!

~

From written correspondence to phone and in-person conversations, hiring managers want to determine whether you are a) the best possible candidate or raw material for the job and b) a good fit for the team and the organization. Words describing how excellent you are have little essence. While interviews are about you (at least in part), they are really about the value that you will bring to your prospective employer.

Some job seekers have a tendency to use very colorful words and phrases to describe themselves. They range from: *outstanding, excellent,* and *terrific* to *remarkable* and *the best possible, perfect choice.* Such words appear first in correspondence, the reading of which makes hiring teams fade away like spring flowers after the return of subzero temperatures. This fading continues when they hear the same messages by phone and in person.

As a job candidate you have the choice of letting your credentials and accomplishments speak, or glorifying yourself verbally. Words of self-love and affection have little impact on hiring teams. If anything, they are an incredible turnoff. If you are a person with an aura of "you know that you love me" or the attitude of "Maxi me...me, me, me..." you are not the hiring manager's best friend. Tell them what you have done and what you can and will do, as opposed to telling them how great you are. Beyond that, modesty is a quality that is back in vogue, and self-glorifying and self-indulgent candidates are really out of date.

Action point:
- If you have a choice between accomplishing something significant or spending time learning how to interview, consider choosing the former.

68
I Have No Flaws and Have Never Failed

Interviewers will put you on the spot and ask you to talk about your failures. These are situational or behavioral questions. What hiring teams want to see is what kind of challenges you have encountered and how you dealt with them. You will be asked to provide details and not just a high-level overview. Hiring teams know that there are plenty of bad and ugly things that happen during various assignments and team work situations. That's what they want to hear about.

If your answer is that you have never been through any tough and challenging situations, the likely conclusion is that it is simply not true, that you do not want to talk about something unpleasant, or that you simply have not done much in your life and therefore did not encounter challenging circumstances. Would you want to hire a person who has never faced a challenge? Probably not. Every job requires dealing with problems and uncertainty, and some ability to figure things out and do it fast. These situations also test your common sense, and sadly, common sense is no longer common.

You will be evaluated on how you dealt with the situation, what role you played in it, what the outcome was, and what lessons you learned. What will be particularly interesting to your prospective employer is how you influenced the outcome and the longer-term lessons you learned. If you failed at something and talk about it openly, it does not automatically mean that you won't get a job. If there were lessons to learn from it and you learned nothing and did not apply anything to future situations, that's a cause for a no.

Action point:
- To get comfortable talking about your failures, you will need to practice.

69

Yeah, I Have Been Told That Before...

To continue the subject of learning from experience and making ongoing improvements, let me add that employers need employees who will continue to evolve along with the organization. As one executive noted: "How many people see things that do not work and know what does not work, yet only complain and do nothing to make things better? What we need are people who can actually do something about problems."

My team interviewed a candidate who was interested in a commercial banking career, which often starts with a job as a credit analyst. A knowledge of accounting is essential to being successful in this role. This candidate indicated that several people mentioned the importance of accounting. Yet he did nothing about it over a one-year period while still interviewing for credit analyst positions. Fast forward a few years, and this will likely be an employee who knows that he needs to pay a lot of attention to details in order not to make a costly lending error, yet will do nothing about it. Nobody wants *that* employee.

If you have been told about your shortcomings – even agree with the assessment – and do nothing to improve, what the hiring manager hears is: "I lack the ability to learn, to make positive changes, to make improvements, and to utilize willpower. You do not want me on your team!"

Action point:
- Develop a system to capture feedback, whether during interviews or beyond. Then work to develop a plan to make lasting changes in your behavior. Research shows that it can take close to a year to make changes stick. Start now.

70

There Has Been a Lot of Negative Press about Your Organization

If you are a candidate who decides to address negative press or other derogatory information about a company with an interviewer who works for that company, slow down and think it through. Confronting hiring team members with questions that may be unpleasant to discuss requires the utmost degree of tact and finesse.

Representatives of a business are, or will behave as, "rah, rah, rah" supporters because that's their job. If they were negative about the place where they work, you would not want to work there. If you catch them after hours and you know them personally, it is remarkable how much more honest people can be. For the purposes of the interview though, they are cheerleaders, and you are not there to put them on the spot.

If you are concerned about an organization's financial condition or adverse publicity, do your homework to determine if there is a fundamental problem with how the business operates. Use your contacts inside and outside the company to get an insight into their challenges. Should you decide to inquire about the issues with an interviewer, think through the wording of your questions ahead of time. Consider referring to a source of your research and ask politely for an opinion. If you can't do the above, consider letting your questions go, but think about whether you want to work there.

Action points:
- Make sure that whatever the data you inquire about is well-researched. It will be a blow to your credibility if your question is based on questionable sources.
- Consider whether you'd react well to a similar inquiry if you were an interviewer.

71
I Really Disagree with You!

~

Not all job hunters have an opportunity to debate an issue and present and defend their points of view. When and if you do, it is important to know how you should behave. The goal is not to engage in a full-scale argument, which is usually inappropriate for an interview setting, and may not do much good in your quest for employment.

Rule # 1 – Never strongly disagree with a member of the hiring team (unless the company welcomes such behavior).

Rule # 2 – Be tactful when expressing any disagreement.

Rule # 3 – Do not dwell on the issue if you still disagree with your potential employer's opinions.

Remember that the interview is not a presidential debate or the Doha Debates broadcast on the BBC. The stronger your opinions are, the more you need to learn to control them and how you express your opposing views. Pushing something just to make a point will not get you far. After all, interviewers typically have an upper hand in the bargaining position and have the right to make an offer or not. People can be very subjective about those who are argumentative. They will immediately think twice about what to expect from you if that's how you behave during the interview.

If you think that you will score points by disagreeing, in the majority of cases you will be wrong. In those few instances when you need to present your solution to a case or business situation, focus on your proposal and its benefits as opposed to just disagreeing. Finally, if you if have ethical or other objections to something being communicated, perhaps it is a red flag. You should think twice before pursuing this particular opportunity.

72

Would You Like a Beer?

~

Of those interviewees who bring notepads with them, few actually take notes. Some individuals may feel that there is nothing to take notes about, which is a mistake. You can get lots of valuable information about a company, prospective job, or the team, which will help with your decision whether to take the job if you are given an offer. The question is if you have the ability to notice good advice and then act on it. You are not interviewing just to chit chat; it is active work before, during, and after! For those who come in just to hang out, I often get an urge to ask if they'd like a beer with their interview.

One part of preparing your notes is what you found during your pre-interview research, including the questions you would like to ask your interviewers. This should not be confused with printing pages after pages about the institutions and people you are meeting with. To an experienced interviewer, it looks like a ploy to impress her or him. People get annoyed by such amateur behavior and may even regard it as lazy. What you should be doing instead is jotting down conclusions and questions that are the result of your homework about the prospective employer – no more than one or two pages.

Members of the interviewing team prepare for interviews: they have your resume, cover letter, and often notes and questions. They are also in an active note-taking mode when speaking with you. How do you think that they will perceive you if you do less work than they do?

Action points:
- A valuable skill to learn is to take notes without looking at what you are writing too much. This helps with maintaining eye contact and having a fluid conversation.
- Engage in interviews by taking notes and follow up on those notes.

73

I Want to Have Your Job by the Age of...

~

It is commendable to have ambition and aspirations. What's not so great for a potential employee is to appear to be naïve or foolish because you say something that is unrealistic and unachievable. In other words, hiring managers can't stand the empty words of underachievers who try to impress their potential employers by talking about their unattainable desires.

The greener you are, the more unsubstantiated your longer-range plans may be, especially if you plan on achieving them within a relatively short period of time. If you are more tenured in your career and have a chance of accomplishing something significant, consider whether your interviewer may be eyeing the same job. For instance, if you are interviewing at a commercial bank with a chief lending officer and declare that you'd like to be the CEO of that organization in ten years, what if she or he actually fancies the same job? That would be awkward, even if you are not likely to get the job before she or he does. Most people are threatened by competition.

If you are asked what you aspire to be doing a few years from now, be aggressive but realistic with your goals. More generic career profiles or jobs are easier to discuss without the organizational context. If you a have a specific plan and may have made progress in reaching your goals, then feel free to share. Be mindful, though, of the job that you are applying for and how your career discussions may impact the perception of your candidacy. Do not lose focus on why you are there.

Action points:
- Consider keeping to yourself career aspirations that are contrary to the role you are applying for.
- Remember that companies first hire you to do the job at hand and only then for what else you may be capable of.

74
Wow, This Is Really Hard to Do

~

During an interview, a job seeker was asked to review a case and provide a solution within a defined period of time. After reviewing the assignment, his first reaction to the hiring manager was that "it was a very hard case." This was not the only mistake the applicant made, but it was a piece of evidence that he could not perform well under pressure. Regardless of your experience levels prospective employers will use various tools to assess how you will behave under pressure.

Whether you are asked to review and analyze a set of financial statements, solve a business task, or tackle an incredibly challenging opportunity, your prospective team members do not want someone who perspires at the mere thought of a challenge. They want a colleague who can face a tough situation with a positive attitude and solve that problem. It is critical for a hiring team to weed out those who can't deal with stress and pressure. As noted previously, if this is how you behave during interviews, what should the hiring team expect from you once you are on the job?

If you find that the glimpses of what's to come are not something you can handle, then it may be a good time to face the fact that the job may not be the right fit for you. It is very important to be honest with yourself and not let hopes or the allure of a good salary cloud your judgment. Consider getting out of the running sooner rather than later and do not ignore warning signs.

Action point:
- When facing a challenging situation during the application process, your reaction will be closely evaluated. You have to be prepared to handle stresses from both the appearance and performance points of view.

75

Let Me Give You a Sample of My Work

~

Let me give you a sample of my work and … it really sucks! Interviewers will never cease being baffled by job applicants who are given a rare opportunity to present themselves in the best possible light, including providing a sample of their work, and blow it. It begs the question: If you have the time necessary to prepare properly, why do you fail to put the needed effort into ensuring the highest quality product? Why would you want to submit an inferior sample of your work? Is this just to help eliminate your candidacy and get a thank-you note from your competition?

Credit analysts in commercial banking are often asked to provide a sample of their analytical work – an example of their analysis. Not uncommonly, interviewers find problems with the quality of their business writing, including grammatical and punctuation errors, spreadsheet errors, and analytical flaws. This work is a chance to demonstrate the final product of the analyst's labor. A poorly written analysis sends only one message: do not hire me!

Be mindful, however, that your other actions do not introduce contradictions in your work sample. For instance, if you are providing a written sample but your other communications, such as cover letters or e-mails, are riddled with flaws, then the hiring team may dismiss them or put less emphasis on stronger elements. Anything you do has to be consistent throughout.

Action points:
- If you can't provide an impeccable example of your work, you should not be applying for jobs.
- Make sure that the example of work is yours, or you risk tarnishing your reputation when the truth comes out (and it usually does).

76
Do You Have a Card?

~

Frequently, an applicant will forget to ask a member of the interviewing team for a business card. Imagine a situation when you ask but the interviewer does not have one. You proceed to wrap things up, shake hands, thank her or him for the opportunity, and head out. The interviewer's reaction? *So you already put your note-pad away and did not even bother to ask for my e-mail address. You are either too lazy to pull your pen back out and ask an extra question in order to drop a follow-up note, or you simply lack the intelligence to ask the next-step question if the answer to your first question is no.* Either way, the reaction does not bode well for you.

While e-mail, IM, texting, and other means of communication are ever-present, business professionals still use business cards in most companies and industries (for now). Asking for one is still a norm of business etiquette. If you do not ask for one or otherwise do not obtain the contact information you need to follow up with a thank-you note, it can deduct a point or two from your candidacy. Where these points will matter even more is when your competitors do what they are supposed to do. If you are neck-and-neck with other candidates, imagine losing out on a job offer because you lost a few simple points here and there – something that could have been avoided without any effort. We see this happen all the time when meeting with candidates.

Action points:
- Asking for a business card should be a standard point in your interview "checklist" (unless it is not something your industry does).
- It is your obligation to follow up with an interviewer to thank her or him. An extra point of contact is an extra opportunity to develop a positive impression and rapport.

77

Do You Have a Lot of Old People?

There are many generational differences in today's workforce. For example, by some account my industry, commercial banking, has four generations working side by side for the first time in its history. This generational coexistence can at times cause misunderstandings and even tensions. Yet the situation can also offer incredible opportunities to develop and to learn from more experienced colleagues.

If you are a person uncomfortably aware of the ages of and age differences among your colleagues, beware! Some applicants have even asked their interviewers to describe the team compositions and whether team members are young or old. A few companies wear it as a badge of honor that their teams are young, and they advertise it as one of the benefits of working for them. Do not forget that a dynamic culture does not automatically arise from youth. A team could be old, older, or have a mix of team members of various ages. Do not fall into the trap of publicly displaying a belief that youth is an intrinsic benefit to a company.

Naturally, people in different age groups are likely to be different in terms of their values, priorities, and work attitudes. That is no reason to make it the focus of your conversation. You wouldn't like the hiring teams discriminating against you based on your age, would you? So don't do it yourself. Your interviewers could also be considerably older individuals, and they could take your age-related comments personally.

The key advice I can give you is to keep your mouth shut when it comes to age. It is inappropriate to inquire whether your prospective team is largely old or young. It is not about the age of the team but about the culture and environment in which you may get a chance to work.

78
Do You Think I Can Leave Earlier?

~

When you are scheduling an interview or are in the midst of one, unless you decide to do something extreme, such as terminate while in progress and walk out, you will typically be done with the interview when it is over. Interviews run their course, and the hiring team is in charge, determining the timing and scope of interviews.

Here is a story of a job seeker who inquired during the interview if she could see the last and the most senior member of the team earlier so that she could catch an earlier flight. The hiring manager's response was that his schedule had changed, and he could no longer meet with her. She was "free to go." The applicant thought that the interviews were going well and even inquired when she was likely to hear back. As it turns out, that senior manager cancelled his interview after he learned that the applicant was trying to get out early without any true extenuating reason. This was not the commitment he wanted to see in a future team member. A few days later she received a letter declaring no interest in her candidacy.

Certainly there are some rare instances of personal and other emergencies that may warrant asking to be excused from an interview and that may entitle you to a rescheduling. Outside of those occasions, you are at the mercy of a prospective employer, and business etiquette will require you to hang tight, be patient, and not ask for something that might otherwise knock you out of the running.

Action point:
- As a hopeful potential employee, your responsibility is to be as flexible as you can be through the entire application process. Anything short of that can put your employment opportunity in jeopardy.

79
I Have a Harder Time Finding Common Ground with Women

~

Just like references to age during the application process and in interviews in particular, there are other off-limits topics. They are potentially discriminatory and unacceptable to discuss. One of them is gender. The list also includes religion, race, ethnicity, sexual orientation, and even politics.

As an example, over the years I encountered several individuals who made general remarks and comparisons of women versus men during interviews, but one individual stood out in particular. He inquired about the composition of the team, including how many men we had versus the number of women. He later explained that it was difficult for him to maintain a good conversation with female colleagues. He was not good at "talking about dresses, makeup, and other female things." Other than that, he had "good" inter-personal skills and could "work well on any team."

A comment like that made the hiring team imme-diately drop the candidate. There are plenty of women who would not talk about dresses, makeup, and the like – let alone in a professional business setting. Moreover, the team was concerned that this person had issues about working side-by-side with women on the team. Hiring teams are not doctors, but the appli-cant seemed to need some counseling and not just a lesson on what a professional conversation should include.

Action points:
- Avoid topics that may be offensive and sound discriminatory to a hiring team.
- Stay focused on the purpose of the interview: showcasing your talents and learning about the needs of the team.

80
I Have No Idea How to Do It - Teach Me

~

Unless a prospective work opportunity includes training for individuals with no prior experience, you will be expected to bring a set of skills and expertise with you. However, some applicants find it acceptable to offer assurances that they can learn on the job, if proper training is offered.

Nobody has the precise skills and training needed for the job anymore. Candidates come from diverse backgrounds. The task for a hiring team is to identify transferable skills and experiences that will allow a person to be successful at her or his job. Successful applicants help prospective employers to identify those skills and determine how they are likely to translate into successful performance.

If you are applying for a job and nothing in your prior experiences can bring you close to proving that you can do the job well, a question begs to be asked about what you are doing at the interview and whether you read the job description. Why would a company want to spend its employees' time looking for someone with experience if it could just hire an inexperienced candidate for very little money? Unless you can help a company answer those questions, it may be challenging to prove why you are the right candidate for the job.

Action points:

- Unless applying for a job that includes formal training, be careful about declaring that you will do the job well *if* you are provided with proper training. The team will not need your particular candidacy then. Anyone would do.
- Create a clear link between what you have done so far and what the prospective job requires. This will give you a chance to prove that you will thrive as a member of the team.

81

I Am Looking for a Fun, Relaxing Environment

~

I am looking for a fun, relaxing environment where I can grow as quickly as possible. This or something similar is what recruiters hear from some candidates. The disconnect is in the fact that a balanced lifestyle is rarely associated with fast growth. You have to pick which one you want. Do you want to have lots of fun, or do you want to grow?

Every interview is an exchange of messages from which recruiting teams work to identify the "best" candidate, and candidates determine whether the opportunity is the right one for them. All too often, once candidates apply, they proceed to accept an offer if the price is right. Where they fail is in listening for clues about what the job and work culture of the prospective employer are like and what kind of work ethic and commitment will be expected of them.

Ultimately, work can be fun, but it does not mean that it will be relaxing. You will need to decide for yourself whether you are a high achiever who will work extremely hard in a job that requires many sacrifices or if you are happy with having a balanced lifestyle with limited growth and a more modest earning potential. Once you do, adjust your expectations accordingly and do not be frustrated if you are not getting the opposite.

Do not forget that your message is important, and interviewers will be listening for which end of the spectrum you aspire to achieve. If they communicate to you that the job will require evenings, weekends, and working whatever hours needed, they will likely pass on your candidacy if you tell them that you'd like to spend more time with your family and work more or less "regular," daytime hours.

82

Let Me Tell You about My Dog

~

In order to fully understand a candidate, many interviewers go beyond the world of business and try to get a
glimpse of your personal world. What do you like to do
outside of work? What are your hobbies? What types of
community involvement do you participate in?

Some people like to do pottery. Others enjoy travel.
Some are into fishing. And still others are into martial
arts. Anything unusual – and particularly, memorable
– can potentially play to your benefit because you will
stand out in the minds of prospective employers. If
you have lots of strengths on the professional side plus
unique or outstanding achievements on the personal
side, you can be the well-rounded and unique candidate that organizations will remember.

Nonetheless, "memorable" does not mean unethical, eyebrow-raising, or potentially polarizing. If you have some gray areas in your private life, keep them to yourself, and let's hope that the Internet is not going to give you away. Riots after a sports event, participation in an adult movie, or even engagement in a divisive political event are probably not things that you want to advertise, unless your industry and employer welcomes that kind of profile. Sometimes people ask, "What if I feel very passionate about this issue?" I'd answer with a question: "Do you care more about demonstrating your convictions or about getting the job?" The choice is yours.

Lastly, manage the amount of information, including deciding if it is too trivial. Just like a candidate who kept going on and on about her dog, his habits and lifestyle, the role he played in her life, and other details, job seekers need to remember why they are at an interview, and that everything is good in moderation. Your personal details can quickly turn into your enemy.

83

Yikes, 25 Percent Writing?

~

Among the various skills that a successful applicant has to possess, self-awareness stands out as an important quality. It means paying attention to your own facial expressions, gestures, posture, and other body language. If they are left unchecked, you could end up like a candidate who interviewed for a position as a junior credit analyst on my former team. He inquired about the typical day of an analyst and was told that analysts spend at least 25 percent of their time on writing analyses. The candidate's reaction was a frown of disdain and disapproval, accompanied by a "yikes." His negative reaction (which he was oblivious to), along with a few other conclusions, cost him a job offer. He was not interested in an essential component of work that every analyst has to do, nor did he know how to react properly to undesirable information.

This is one of numerous examples of occasions when facial and other expressions, if left unchecked, can result in rather detrimental outcomes. You get only a limited amount of time to interact with interviewers, and you don't get a second chance. They will not do a debrief with you or ask what you meant by your pouting, blowing air between your lips in what may have been viewed as boredom, or frowning. They will likely assume the worst because they do not have the luxury of time to give you another chance: They have many other applicants to evaluate and very little time.

Action points:
- Examine yourself in front of a mirror, paying attention to your facial expressions, mimicry, and gestures.
- Ask others to observe you and point out if you have bad habits in your body language that may be inappropriate during interviews.

84
How Much Are You Paying?

~

Compensation is typically not something that comes up early in the interviewing process. It is generally considered to be a discussion reserved for when an offer is extended to you. You may be able to get a salary range if a company discloses this information (this is rare); if external recruiters give you an indication; or if hiring teams mention salary expectations earlier on because they feel that you might be too expensive, to avoid wasting their time and yours. If your salary requirements are within an acceptable range, they will proceed with the interview process. Experienced hiring teams will find out about your current salary and your expectations through an application or during earlier conversations.

Beyond these situations, there is a high probability that a direct inquiry about salary will be considered as putting the cart ahead of the horse. Some hiring teams may feel that you are being presumptuous about your chances of getting the job, if you are already talking about money. This is a game of patience. Money discussion is the reward for being in the running and potentially being a finalist.

Your goal is to learn about the range so that you can better plan your negotiations. This is where your in-company network may be of value, or having a general understanding of the industry ranges for that type of job. You will frequently run into an unwillingness to give you much more than a modest percentage over your current salary, even if the salary band allows much higher pay. For instance, the percentage increase is ten to twenty percent in my industry of commercial banking. This is when knowing the actual range comes in handy so you will know how much you can push. Overall, be aware of when it is appropriate to have salary discussions and do not cross the line too early. Salary negotiation is a valuable skill and outside the scope of this book.

85
I Have Done This and That and That

We all have distinct career paths. Yet many of us will not be working in the same capacity for long periods of time. Employee mobility continues to rise as it has over the last couple of decades. We get a chance to do a variety of jobs over shorter and shorter periods of time. It is also becoming more acceptable to jump around from company to company. Still, employers want to see some mid- to longer-term direction, even though it may evolve and change over time. The longer you have been in the work force, the greater this expectation is.

If you are an individual who has done a little bit of this and a little bit of that, you need to come to an interview prepared to explain and even defend your career choices. Moreover, you need to establish to your interviewers that the job you are interviewing for is not going to be one where you will try to determine what you'd like to do "when you grow up." The only exception to this could be if it's one of your first jobs out of school or college, but even then the candidates who have better clarity and direction stand a better chance.

Do not expect your interviewers to fish information out of you about why that particular employment opportunity is something you are a good match for and why you will be successful. They do not have time or patience for helping you determine your career direction. For that, you have books, career offices, advisors, and other sources.

Action points:
- Ask experienced interviewers to review your resume to identify gaps, short-duration jobs, and lack of career direction or progression.
- Practice persuasive and reasonable explanations to support your career choices.

86
Oh Merde, Pardon My French

~

Some interviewers can make you very comfortable and relaxed and set a pace for a casual conversation. When that happens, you can never relax completely and allow yourself to do what the interviewer is doing. They are interviewers for a reason and can do many things that you can't. Even if a hiring team member uses casual or stronger language (let's hope this does not happen as it is not professional), it does not mean that you should lower yourself to the same level.

The best guidance is to stay true to yourself and your style as well as to remain within the norms of appropriate behavior. Don't forget to watch your language. There is absolutely no place in the business setting of an interview for stronger expressions; even softening them with "pardon my French" does not grant you permission to cross the line into the realm of the unacceptable.

From the moment you begin applying and interacting with hiring teams, you have your brand to establish, maintain, and control. Your image has to be as impeccable as it can be if you want to increase your chances for success. While some adjustments for the interviewer's pace and tone are warranted, this does not mean that you have to emulate her or him completely. When you do, you may signal that you have no backbone of your own and are willing to do anything to please.

Action points:
- Regardless of the behavior of the interviewers, you have to maintain the highest standard for your own actions during interviews.
- Remember that slang, strong expressions, cursing, and casual and other inappropriate language is off limits during interviews.

87
I Would Love to Get Together after Work

Unless you knew the interviewer before you started the application process or unless she or he invites you for a meal outside the office, you should not be meeting a member of the interviewing team outside the interview setting. Some hiring teams may meet with candidates for breakfast, lunch, or dinner. There is usually nothing inappropriate about that. However, if you get a sense that a meeting has more of a personal nature or you are not comfortable with it, you can always turn down the invitation.

Some applicants – fortunately, they are a minority – have been known to surprise interviewers by asking to meet at later time to continue the conversation. The goal was to get to know the interviewer better and to positively influence the decision outcome. Setting aside interviewing etiquette and the fact that it is inappropriate for an applicant to seek an additional audience, members of the hiring team are in positions of authority. Meeting with an applicant outside of work in a social setting will likely introduce a conflict of interest. Moreover, it will be considered inappropriate and unprofessional behavior.

If you are a very social person who has few boundaries or who tries to be entrepreneurial in how you get a job, you need to focus on building internal limits. Keep your professional life separate from anything that has a hint of personal life.

Action point:
- If you'd like to build a better business relationship with one of your interviewers, wait until the decision is rendered. Then the question is if the interviewer would like to network with you thereafter, especially if you did not get the job.

88
So How Did You Like Me?

~

Hiring managers who have done their jobs for a while sometimes feel they have seen it all. Yet there are always new anomalies and even shockers popping up now and then. Some even wonder what the next strange or outrageous thing a candidate does will be. One of those strange actions is asking an interviewer for immediate feedback about your candidacy and especially how you did during the interview.

First of all, this is not an episode of HGTV's *House Hunters International*, where a real estate broker asks the client what she or he thought of the property. Secondly, you may get a sense during the interview of whether or not the interviewers are impressed with your background. Thirdly, there are usually several contenders for a job. So-called stack-ranking is done after the interviews are wrapped up, unless there is a clear front-runner. As a consequence, interviewers may not know exactly how you are doing compared to others. Lastly, unless the interviewer is the one making hiring decisions, she or he is not going to tell you "yes" because someone else on the team may disagree. No interviewer wants to give false hope and misinformation. On the opposite side, people do not want to have an uncomfortable conversation regarding why you are an inadequate candidate.

Once in a while, prospective employers may interrupt the interview and declare that your experiences do not match what they are looking for. Outside of those instances, interviews, at least for the time being, are not a computer game where you get immediate feedback. If anything, you will probably be labeled as "that" person if you ask for an evaluation during your interview.

89

Give Me Some Dirt on Your Company

~

Maybe it is the inquisitive nature of today's interviewees, in combination with fewer and fewer social boundaries in general, that leads some applicants to quiz hiring teams about their company's challenges. Beyond the behavior of the candidates described in a prior chapter on negative press and financial challenges, some job contenders venture further, into the territory of asking hiring teams for an insider's perspective on gossip and organizational dirt.

A limited number of interviewers will feel comfortable discussing this information. Their answers will likely be in the realm of what's already in the public domain or rather generic details. Otherwise, such information is confidential, and the hiring team is under no obligation to disclose it to you. Even more important is the fact that they are there to sell you on an opportunity, just as you are there to sell your candidacy. It is not in their interest to discuss the organization's challenges.

Lastly, be aware of how you approach this matter. Tread very carefully with questions that are confidential and too close to the skin. It is easy to rub people the wrong way and become known as a candidate who lacks tact. If you truly want to find out dirt about the inside culture of your prospective employer, your internal network is the only means by which to obtain this kind of information. Just make sure that your contacts do not provide feedback to the hiring manager.

Action points:
- If you have a reputation for lacking tact and for being too direct, have a couple of experienced individuals review your questions ahead of time.
- Make a list of topics that you will not venture into so that you can memorize them in preparation for interviews.

90
It's Time to Ask Questions

~

While some interviewers may allow you to ask questions at the beginning or throughout the interview, it is customary to allow applicants to ask questions at the very end. Unfortunately, at times interviews last too long, leaving no time for you to query your interviewers.

Questions are an opportunity for you to learn, clarify, and stand out. Do not ask your interviewers identical questions though. This will likely signal to them that you have no other questions, cannot adapt to changes in circumstance during the interview, and do not use your time wisely trying to learn as much as possible. Unless you are running a public opinion poll and want reliable information from the entire sample, there is not much value in polling all your interviewers for the same information.

Create a list of questions ahead of time based on your research, but cross off those that may have been addressed as you go through the interview process or add new ones as you continue your conversation. If some questions have risen in priority, move them to the top of the list. The list should be a living and breathing organism that continues to evolve as your interviews progress.

Lastly, capture information that is of value or needs to be followed up on. A college student I interviewed was involved in developing a sustainable, multiyear effort for transfer students. During our discussion of his game plan, I shared numerous ideas on how to bring structure and continuity to the group's efforts. Despite having a prime opportunity to capture actionable tips, this individual simply listened and nodded. He did not take a single note. Instead of finishing strong and using the last few minutes to leave a lasting impression, he closed with a passive demeanor and by asking a few boring questions.

AFTER THE INTERVIEW

91
Follow-up – Thank You!

~

I hope that the first thing that you do after completing your interviews is to work on thank-you notes. It is not only an expectation and proper etiquette but also an opportunity to have an extra contact point with your prospective employer, an opportunity to reaffirm your interest in the position (if you are interested), and a chance to stand out from your competitors. At a minimum, you will create a positive impression for the future, since interviewers are potential members of your network.

While formats for your thank-you notes vary, they should contain a salutation, the message, and the closing. Standard template thank-you notes are sad and lack personality. Adding your personal style and something relatable to the meeting with that individual (another reason to take notes) can make you more memorable when members of the interviewing team get together to rank their candidates. Don't forget to thank them for the opportunity and for their consideration. Lastly, keep your communication concise.

Hand-written notes are something few people do, but they are always the most memorable. Just make sure that the reader can decipher your writing. I recommended that a friend of mine who works for a biotech firm send handwritten notes. She was resistant at first because it is not something people do in her industry, but then she did it.

Colleagues who interviewed her for an internal job were buzzing for weeks after they received her notes, because it is not heard of in her industry; instead, a thank-you e-mail was occasionally received. Because it can take days for a handwritten note to be delivered, you may want to immediately send an e-mail as well. Don't worry about it being two notes. If one does not reach the recipient, the other will.

92
Follow-up - Status Update

~

The next type of update and point of contact with the hiring team is following up on the status of your application. This is where you will need to marshal lots of patience. Many organizations are notorious for dragging their feet through the entire application process, including post-interviews. Commonly, if you are out, they will let you know pretty quickly. Otherwise, no news likely means good news.

Some candidates get too worked up thinking about what the lack of updates means, whether they are still in the running, and what chances they might have, and they try to interpret every little action of prospective employers. If you know that you have done your best and more during the interviews, it is time to let the hiring team do its job and focus on other opportunities.

I hope that somewhere in the course of applying you have inquired about the next steps and the timelines. Depending on the answer, you can plan your follow-ups. Most typically, you can follow up in one to two weeks after completing the interviews. Your follow-up serves two purposes: a) getting an update as well as reinforcing your interest in the opportunity and b) refreshing your connection with the hiring team.

In both your message and frequency of follow-ups you want to make sure that you do not pester and do not overdo it. Your inquiry should be respectful, interested, genuine, and brief. Maintaining interest and periodic communication has been known to make candidates stand out among others with similar credentials because they were really interested in an opportunity. As a reminder though, do not overdo your follow-ups. There is nothing more annoying than a desperate or pestering candidate. This is when applicants lose appeal – no matter how strong they are.

93

Where Are Your Heads at?

~

If you are able to call a member of the hiring team for a follow-up, that is better than e-mails, letters, or other forms of communication. However, calls are not as customary. People may be taken aback, unless you have their permission to call and make a prior arrange-ment. It also helps to have a really strong mastery of brief phone conversations. They can be quite powerful in maintaining rapport with hiring teams. Note that I mentioned *maintaining* rapport; it is extremely difficult to build a relationship post-interview.

If possible, try not to leave voice mails. However, it is not always possible. Most voice mails cause more harm than benefit because ever since we "mastered" the e-mail, we traded this "mastery" for the ability to talk by phone and leave voice mail messages. If you want your voice mail to truly count, remember to keep it under twenty to thirty seconds. You should include your name, context (or why you are calling), what you are asking for, and a good concluding remark, including a thank-you and your phone number. Speak your number slowly and repeat it. Don't forget to practice before calling in order to leave a worthwhile message.

When leaving a voice mail, you have to be very careful with every single word. If you are not, you will end up like an applicant I had the displeasure of interviewing. He called two team members, audibly unhappy because it was taking us a bit longer than he expected to make a decision about him. Other than asking for a call back, he wanted to know "where our heads were at," a phrase that is too colloquial, more appropriate for addressing his buddies, and disrespectful under the given circumstances. For a moment, the cynics in us wanted to respond and comment on "where our heads really were." Our professionalism and self-control prevailed, and our decision about this candidate was swift and not in his favor.

94
Do I Qualify Now?

~

A part of your post-interview follow-up (whether formal or informal) is applying lessons learned from the entire interview process. If you are smart about these lessons, you will take them beyond the context of a particular job. It could be that you learned about a particular industry and began targeting a particular role or figuring out how to apply your current experiences and make them transferable to the next role.

I recall approaching an internal candidate who was interested in becoming a credit analyst; mind you, this could have been an external candidate and a person applying for any other job, not just in commercial banking. After reviewing his background, I pointed out that he did not have any of the key prerequisite experiences and did not qualify. We talked for a while, and I gave him lots of tips on how to gain some of the essential

199

experiences in order to be considered for the job in the future. One of those experiences was to learn the fundamentals of accounting and financial statement analysis.

Instead of having a strategy for how to get to the next level, he decided to pay for a quick, online self-study course. He then contacted me to share his "accomplishment" and inquire if he now qualified for the job. Given the scope of that kind of training and the lack of practice that other, longer and more thorough programs could have provided, the answer was a "no" again. He then went back and did something fairly similar and came back with the same question once again. He clearly ignored my advice on gaining relevant experience, such as taking a week-long, in-person course that I recommended and then practicing weekly how to read financial statements to build out his skill set. This was the final drop in concluding that he did not have enough intelligence, maturity, and ability to follow any advice. My team decided to not consider his candidacy again.

95

Desperado

~

There is a fine line between showing interest in an opportunity, at times a strong interest, and really overdoing it. This applies to any stage of your job search but especially to the post-interview stage. Sometimes there are clear and distinct front-runners. In those instances decisions are already made, even before interviews are over, barring discovery of some material derogatory information about an applicant. In many instances, however, there are several leading candidates. It is the small points that will get one of them across the finish line. Overdoing your interest in a job is something that can cost you the job, because it will come across as desperate, whether you intend it to or not.

Some examples of desperate behavior are frequent follow-ups to check the status of one's application and language that shows you are trying to please and would do anything for the job. Avoid excessive excitement that should be saved for later when you get the job and celebrate with your family and friends. This is not to say that you should not communicate to your prospective employer that you are really interested in a job. Yet, you can do it with grace and self-respect.

You should pay attention to the language in your communication: be polite, professional, and even excited to a degree, but do not beg or act subservient. On the opposite side, for those who fear appearing needy, you should also be careful about not appearing standoffish because that can and will be interpreted as a lack of interest. Be strategic with your follow-ups, including frequency and timing. Double and triple check your language in written communications and pay close attention to your verbal communications.

96
He Is Not Getting a *No*

〜

Nobody wants to hear a no and be rejected when applying for a job. I have even heard people say that they did not really care for a particular job and most likely would have turned it down, but that it would have been great to have received an offer. Imagine if you really want and need a job – a no in those instances can be crushing.

As part of getting closure, some candidates want feedback about why they were rejected. As a hiring manager, even during interviews you often really want to give feedback to an applicant whom you like, have sympathy for, or otherwise would have liked to help. Yet, interviewers do not do this for several reasons. One such reason is the risk, however real or imagined, of law suits and potential legal liability. Another reason is that members of the hiring team just do not have the time and resources to do it; they are kept very busy with their own jobs. Any proper feedback conversation should and will take at least thirty minutes or more. The last – but by far not the least – reason is not wanting to open a Pandora's box of endless discussions.

Some interviewers have tried to be helpful to a prospect who did not get a job and provided feedback. In the majority of these cases, interviewers swore never to do it again. The reasons ranged from candidates pleading for them to reconsider the decision to arguing that the feedback was not correct and trying to contest it. These situations turn ugly very quickly, and people who wanted to do something good for applicants swore to never attempt it again. If you really need feedback, your best chance is to have a business or personal relationship with someone on the inside. Ask to be coached on how to improve as opposed to asking for feedback specific to applying for a particular job. Your "coaches" are more likely to be honest. Otherwise, just let it go and move on.

97

I Am Not Happy

~

Similar to arguing, which was discussed earlier, expressing displeasure of any kind to a prospective employer is not something you'd want to do when applying for a job. As emotional as a job search and career decisions can be, you have to keep your emotions in check, including any expressions of negativity.

One of numerous applicants comes to mind. She applied for a job with my former team and was waiting for a decision after two rounds of interviews. Although she was not our first choice, she was a solid runner-up. My team needed a few more days to decide if we were going to extend an offer to our first choice and how much we were able to offer. In the meanwhile, the runner-up was getting impatient, leaving voice mails for me and for another team member to check on the status of the process. It was clear from her tone that she was annoyed by the lack of a decision, not realizing that it was actually good news for her because we were still keeping her in mind.

After hearing another unhappy message about her "not being sure where we were and what we were doing," we steadfastly sent a letter of no interest. The job she was applying for required, among other skills, a considerable amount of patience and professionalism – skills she clearly she did have.

Whether the recruiting team is running behind schedule or not getting back to you as quickly as you would like, there are many ways to follow up in a professional, respectful, and patient manner. When you express negative emotions, you may get kicked out of the running. If you like to be in control, you will need to realize that the job search is not something you will have control over. At a minimum, you need to share the driver's seat. Displeasure should never be in your bag of tricks.

98
Making up Salary Information

~

Although some employers may reach out to their net-works for informal background inquiries, background verification usually formally occurs after you accept an offer and before you start on the job. Your employment will likely be contingent on satisfactory background checks and other follow-up actions. In addition to background checks, some HR departments can call your former employers to verify whether you worked there, whether you left on good terms, and what your salary level was. These inquiries can vary based on the company's practices and what's permitted in the state where the company operates.

Salaries can be verified too. Based on anecdotal knowledge, some job seekers routinely inflate their actual income, running the risk of being caught being dishonest. In general, businesses will pay you based on the established salary range or band for your type of job. These ranges can be rather broad and are driven by your level of experience and qualifications. Your current compensation level can be another determinant. Especially if you are currently employed, a prospective employer will likely offer you more money than you are currently making in order to attract you. If your current compensation is materially below the range a prospective employer offers, the company may be inclined to give you more but not nearly as much as the range permits.

This is why some job seekers are inclined to overstate their salary, in hopes that they will get an increase to the "current" level of compensation. Do not forget, however, that it is risky, and I'd recommend being honest. Do not be surprised if an offer is rescinded when salary verification is made and the number is found to be materially different from what you stated.

99
I Am Not Sure If I Am Interested

~

Once the interview is over, you should already know if you are interested in the job, if the price is right. While the compensation package is an important determinant, if you are not intrigued enough by the company, team, growth opportunity, or industry, you should consider pulling out and not wasting people's time. If you want to make someone's blacklist, being wishy-washy is the way to do it after a hiring team spent time vetting you. Are you in or out? Take the time to make your decision, but you have to be decisive.

Sooner or later in the process, certain employers may ask if you are interviewing somewhere else. You should be honest about it but do not voluntarily spill out all the information and which companies they are. Employers typically would want to know this to better manage the interview and offer process. This may also be indicative that you are a stronger contender, and that they want to work around your schedule. Employers won't like that you are still waiting to see how other interviews play out, but usually they would give you a bit more time.

The message about why you are pulling out before or after an offer is made to you is just as important. It has to be something real and reasonable and must show that you are mature about your career decisions. Individuals do not like to be passed on, and neither do businesses. The only difference is that companies tend to have more options and can move to plan B, if they know that plan A is not happening.

Action points:
- Treat your prospective employers how you'd like to be treated or, better yet, how they'd like to be treated.
- Put yourself in the potential employer's shoes: if you'd feel you were in the dark, chances are that they will too.

100
A Graceful Exit

Should you decide to exit the application process, you have to have a clear communication strategy and do damage control. Chances are that you will meet or even work with the same people again. Companies tend to stick around, but people change jobs. If you do not handle the situation with the utmost professionalism, people will remember. If you handle the situation well, you will stand out from the sea of candidates, and that can benefit you in the future.

When I interviewed with a couple of commercial banks some years ago, I decided to pass on one of two offers. It was a similar job to what I was doing before, for just a bit more pay. The growth opportunities were unclear and no next-level corporate title that one would expect in commercial banking. I opted for a more challenging job, clearly out of my comfort zone, even though the pay was about the same.

I first had a very extensive conversation with the HR recruiter to explain my decision. It was rational and well-justified. I did not get defensive just because another company was trying to prove why they were a better choice. I had another very extensive conversation with the hiring manager. In addition, I sent personalized letters to all the interviewing team members, thanking them for their time and explaining in brief why I decided to pursue another option. I sent similar notes to three other team members who had met with me, including the CEO.

This same company continued to court me for the next three years for two reasons (by its own admission): I was a candidate they liked quite a bit, and they were impressed by how I handled myself declining their offer. So, if you turn a company down, take the time to do it right.

BONUSES

101
Mapping Strengths and Weaknesses

In Chapter 1 I mentioned an exercise to help you focus on your strengths and minimize the negative impact of one or two key weaknesses. Since each phase of the interview process requires unique skills, consider mapping your strengths and weaknesses. As the next step, identify the actions you should do more of or less of – or those you should perhaps not change at all.

Before the interview

Strength –
Strength –

Weakness –

Strategy* –

During the interview

Strength –
Strength –

Weakness –

Strategy* –

After the interview

Strength –
Strength –

Weakness –

Strategy* –

What you need to do more of as well as less of, how you can make those improvements, and the timeline to reach those goals.

102

Brief Analysis of the Commercial Banking Industry for Prospective Job Seekers

~

Your industry research should include the following: what the industry does, its key players, its key products and services, the key markets it serves, and industry trends and outlook. Do not forget to do your research in the context of companies that you are interviewing with to ensure that your conclusions are connected to the actual situation, and that your research is more than just a compilation of dry data. If your prospective employer is a regional or local company, spend more time on understanding regional or local dynamics and peculiarities that are more likely to impact your prospective employer.

Quality industry analysis always ties the context to a particular company in question (if it contains analysis of specific industry players) and is always drawing conclusions as opposed to reciting facts. In commercial banking we train credit analysts, who perform industry analyses, to ask and think in terms of the "so what" question. The goal is to draw conclusions within industry analyses and determine what the analysis means. The less familiar you are with an industry, the more time and effort you should spend on understanding broader industry dynamics. If you are an experienced industry insider, an understanding of higher, macroeconomic issues is still helpful because this is the type of data executives focus on in performing their daily duties.

※ ※ ※

This industry summary was written in March 2014

Commercial banks in the United States hold an estimated $13 trillion in assets, with another $1 trillion held by savings banks and credit unions. While the overall worldwide banking industry generates an estimated $3.4 trillion in revenue, US commercial banks generate a combined annual revenue of $700 billion. For comparison, the US current-dollar GDP for 2013 was $17 trillion, which means that US commercial banking revenue equates to a modest 4.1% of the US economy. If we look at the top industries of the US economy, the commercial banking sector (as part of finance and insurance, accounting for 6.6% of the GDP) is closing the list of the top five industries, with the top three being real estate and rental and leasing (12.9%), state and local government (9.1%), and healthcare and social assistance (7.1%). The commercial banking sector shares a ranking with durable goods manufacturing.

There are about 6,000 commercial banks as well as 1,000 savings banks and 7,000 credit unions in the US. Yet the majority of the industry's assets are concentrated with the four largest banks (J.P. Morgan Chase, Bank of America, Citigroup, and Wells Fargo), each having greater than $1 trillion in total assets ($8 trillion in aggregate as of September 2013). US commercial banks hold an estimated $13 trillion in combined assets while savings banks and credit unions hold only $1 trillion. If we look at trends over a twenty-year period, the number of FDIC-insured banks declined from 13,221 on December 31, 1993 to 9,181 on December 31, 2003 to 6,812 on December 31, 2013 as a result of consolidations as well as bank failures, mostly during the Great Recession of 2007-2009.

The most elementary banking business model is taking deposits, lending those deposits, and collecting loan payments within the specified timeframe and on the conditions specified, with minimal losses. Therefore, every commercial bank starts with deposit and cash management services. The initial lending business for smaller, community banks is residential lending. As a bank grows, it engages in commercial real estate lending. It is estimated that loans secured by real estate (residential and commercial) accounted for about 52% of total lending in September 2013. The next area to develop is what is known as commercial & industrial (C&I) lending, which means extending loans to operating businesses (agricultural, manufacturing, and industrial) that deliver products or services (approximately 20% of total lending). The rest of lending activity is attributed to consumer loans, which account for approximately 17% of the activity, and all other loans, approximately 11%. The next evolution in banking lines of business could include investment management and trust services, specialty banking businesses (i.e. lending by more specific industry and loan type, such as nonprofit lending, private banking, leasing, credit cards, auto loans, student loans, and others), and even diversifying into non-banking services, such as insurance. As banks grow, loan sizes and the quantity of clients grow. Geographic focus, risk tolerance, and many other parameters change and evolve also.

As the US economy continues to stabilize and employment numbers improve, the industry continues to recover. The commercial banking business is highly cyclical, impacted by economic fluctuations. Interest rates, consumer spending, and the real estate housing market are the key components of economic health. If you look at the statements of income and expenses of an average bank, you find two key components: 1) Net Interest Income (net difference between what banks earn on loans and pay on deposits) and 2) Noninterest Income (e.g. banking fees) and Noninterest Expenses, the most typical of which are salaries, benefits, technology, rent, and insurance.

The Net Interest (spread) for banks as of the third quarter of 2013 was 3.26%, which shows the percentage banks earn between making loans and paying interest on deposits. This is a rather narrow profit margin for a business to operate with, especially if it still needs to pay employees and cover various other overhead expenses. This is why banks are typically risk-averse. All they can lose is two to three dollars on every hundred dollars that they lend. That's it. There is not much room for error! Much more beyond that and banks can sustain significant losses or even go out of business, unless the government bails them out. But let's leave that contentious topic out of this book's industry summary.

Firstly, during a downturn, interest rates go down, and banking's Net Interest Income gets compressed, leading to lower profits. Secondly, as borrowers struggle during downturns and some go out of business, banks lose money on loans, which can lead to banks posting net losses and even going out of business. Additionally, fewer creditworthy companies and individuals are left in the marketplace. Credit standards tighten, and banks become very selective in extending credit. Borrowers become debt-averse. All this significantly reduces the flow of loans to banks. Depositors run away from stock markets and other forms of investment and instead rush back to banks with their deposits and hoard their cash (even if banks already pay very little in interest and much less when the economy is down). As such, "the juices of the economy" are not flowing. Banks are sitting on mounds of cash that are not able to earn any money for them. In turn, banks pay very low interest to depositors. Net Interest Margins for banks get compressed, and they need to watch and sometimes cut their overhead. That's a lose-lose proposition over extended periods of time.

During the economic recovery that we are experiencing in 2014 as this book is being written, loan growth is on the rise. Banks have been able to clean their balance sheets of bad loans and those that have survived are able to show much stronger capital and liquidity. By some accounts, regional and local banks did better than the large national banks during the Great Recession.

Despite some positive trends – such as declining write-offs (net of charge-offs), slowly rising interests rates, and therefore net interest margins – bank revenues and net profits have been growing at a snail's pace in the last four years. A flat yield curve (the difference between short- and long-term interest rates), increased costs of regulatory compliance, loss of or shrinkage in once-profitable lines of business (such as credit cards, student loans, auto loans, and overdraft fees) are some of the reasons for relative stagnation in the industry. Another significant challenge is the hypercompetitive banking environment, where there is anecdotal knowledge that the pricing and aggressive lending terms in commercial lending are now back to their pre-downturn levels. All of this is while economic conditions are not anywhere near as strong as they were in the 2005-2007 time frame. The industry's revenue rebounded 9.3%, to $660 billion from $604B from 2008 to 2009, but then grew at an anemic pace of 0.6% per year.

The commercial banking industry's saving grace will be once interest rates begin to rise. That's what all banks and their executive teams pray for. This will improve their Net Interest Income and other financial performance criteria. However, stiff competition and the growing commoditization of commercial and retail banking (customers like and want better service but do not want to pay for it), increasing regulatory compliance costs in what is already a highly regulated industry, rising costs of technology required to become more efficient and effective, as well as an impending shortage of talent are putting pressure on banks to become more nimble, to consolidate, and to compete more effectively.

Regulations are already a very substantial and growing expense item for banks. The Consumer Financial Protection Bureau (CFPB), increasing capital requirements (what's known as Basel III's "conservation buffer" of 2.5%, common equity buffer of 2.5%, and global systemically important financial institutions (G-SIFI) or Too-Big-to-Fail institutions required to hold 1% to 2.5% of loss-absorbent capital), the Volker Rule, Regulation E, and many other regulations will continue to put pressure on bank performance, leading to even more consolidation and, by some accounts, to a reduced availability of some products or to the higher cost of others to customers. While the outlook for the industry tends to be moderately positive, it has many challenges ahead.

If your prospective commercial banking employer is operating on a local level, it is also important to look at the local economy and how the bank's customers, the bank proper, and its competitors are faring. For instance, Massachusetts has 152 FDIC-insured banking institutions (which includes commercial banks and savings institutions). Only 47 of them are commercial banks, and the rest are savings banks. This is the opposite of national statistics, where the majority of banks are commercial banks. Only the top five banks ("all" bank FDIC classifications were utilized in this report) have assets greater than $5 billion. The next 30 banks have assets greater than $1 billion, with the remaining majority of banks in MA being small, with assets under $1 billion each. This is representative of the national data, where the majority of assets are "controlled" by the largest institutions.

※※ ※※ ※※

The above should give you a good high-level overview of the industry, and you can dive into specific issues and details, depending on what your line of business will be, your organization's size and market, and numerous other variables.

Beyond industry reports
The next step is to go past the industry reports, if you truly want to understand an industry, its trends, challenges, and opportunities.

Misconception #1: The business of commercial banking is distinctly different from that of investment banking. During the most recent economic crisis, the term *bank* or *banking* was used indiscriminately by the media and politicians, but in many instances, they were referring to investment banks. Commercial banks, on a daily basis, provide a wide range of services, including retail banking through bank branches. These services are essential to keeping companies and individual households running well. Investment banks facilitate and advise on mergers and acquisitions, the issuance of marketable securities, raising other capital, and on other, generally highly transactional, fee-driven services. Yet they cannot hold deposits and lend those deposits.

Misconception #2: Commercial banks are often mistakenly equated to the business of retail branches. Retail branches are an inherent and important part of commercial banks. Yet it is only a part of their business (in many views, retail branch business is a shrinking and potentially disappearing business). At a minimum, the retail banking landscape is expected to change dramatically in the next decade. There is so much more to commercial banks than retail branches, such as their online banking, cash management, and sizable commercial banking activities.

Opportunities for younger generations: One of the most common career paths for growth in the commercial banking business is through becoming a credit analyst. The challenge is that most commercial banks look for trained credit analysts. What we call formal credit training (a full-time training program while getting paid) has been eliminated by the industry in the last ten to twenty years. What's left are a few semi-formal (periodic classroom sessions while working full time) and mostly informal (independent or self-study, on-the-job experience, and through coaching) credit training opportunities. The quality of semi-formal and informal credit training programs varies widely. This is a Catch-22 for many candidates and commercial banks proper because: a) there is a significant need for credit analysts but no systematic training, and 2) there is considerable interest among entry-level candidates in joining banks but no formal credit training available. To exacerbate the problem, most banks do not want to pay for training. Thus, there is a growing need for and shortage of talent.

Another impending talent shortage is among bankers in their thirties and forties. As their more tenured colleagues are retiring in the next ten to twenty years, there is a void of mid-level managers with good leadership experience and training as well as an understanding of how to run a bank on a macro level – beyond the individual teams where these mid-level managers currently operate. If you look at the number of retiring executives and the pure numbers of Baby Boomers, which exceed those of the subsequent generations, there are clear signs of an impending talent shortage, at least in two age and experience groups. This presents significant opportunities for job seekers, if they are able to mitigate and resolve challenges around the lack of training and their own lack of experience.

The information above is more in the realm of an insider's knowledge, not something that would be in the general press. Having a close network of industry professionals will allow you to understand industry dynamics and the dynamics of a specific organization you are applying with.

Sources:
S&P Capital IQ Industry Surveys January 2014, Banking
First Research, Banks and Credit Unions, 2/24/14
The FDIC
The Bureau of Economic Analysis
The OCC's 2013 Survey of Credit Underwriting Practices

103

Behaviors and Qualities Generally Expected during Commercial Banking Interviews

~

There is common interview etiquette that spans companies, industries, and sometimes countries. Yet, some rules of behavior and expectations are specific to particular industries. For example, having a tablet instead of a notepad during interviews is becoming more and acceptable. Yet it is something that will be noted as rather unusual (not in a positive or negative sense, just as unusual) in non-technology-aligned industries. Another example is thank-you notes, and in some industries it is unusual even to get a thank-you blurb via e-mail. In my industry, commercial banking, a formal thank-you letter or a hand-written note is still very much expected.

Below are examples of common expectations in the commercial banking industry in the United States.

- A cover letter is still an expectation, especially when you are not applying through an HR portal.
- Good writing skills are valued, and the lack thereof is viewed negatively.
- Addressing others formally by "Ms." or "Mr." is a standard, unless you are given permission to do otherwise. This is especially applicable when dealing with bankers of an older generation and when corresponding with hiring teams early in the process.
- Being well-dressed and well-groomed is essential.
- Wearing a suit and tie for men and formal business clothes for women is standard. Wearing flip-flops or racy clothes is a candidacy killer.
- Being well-prepared for an interview and having done your homework is just as relevant as it was twenty years ago.
- Being on time is everything, and if you are not early, you are late.
- Having a notepad and pen at interviews is viewed as part of being prepared and professional. Lacking them will place you behind your competition.
- Being actively engaged during interviews, asking questions, and displaying an understanding

of the situation is what quality candidates are expected to do.

- Capturing and then following up on notes is a natural extension of note-taking. Otherwise, why bring a notepad to the interview?
- Sending a thank-you note, preferably a letter or a hand-written note, is something you should still be doing in this industry. It means that you know how to play the game.
- Showing a community focus, interest, and participation is more important than ever.
- It is acceptable to see a moderate degree of job-hopping. If you have been switching jobs too much, it can and will go against you.
- You should have at least some sense and some idea about your longer-term plans and direction.
- Providing references is of value and is important. This is a relatively small industry, and references can be easily verified.

What is standard behavior in your industry?

104
On Being Memorable

~

A good business developer or salesperson makes it her or his goal to ensure that there are a couple of key traits that make her or him memorable. Similarly, as a candidate for a position, you should make it your goal to have two to three accomplishments or traits that you would want your prospective hiring managers to remember you by.

If there are more than two or three, then chances are that you will not be remembered by anything at all. People have limited memories. Hiring teams look at many candidates. Interviewers tend to remember no more than a couple features about you – if any. Thus, before every interview ask yourself what you'd like the prospective recruiting team to remember about you. This does not replace your qualifications as a candidate but rather enhances them. Throughout the interview process, ensure that it is something you put into action. This could be a combination of personal and professional qualities.

For instance, let's suppose that you are originally from a small country that almost no one has heard of or met a person from. That's certainly something that could leave a memorable impression with the hiring team. Another memorable fact could be starting and growing a regional nonprofit organization or owning and operating a sizeable manufacturing company at some point in your career. Lastly, suppose you went into commercial banking after earning a degree in astrophysics and interning for NASA?

There are very many reasons why a recruiting team might find you unique. You need to decide which one or two you want to be remembered by. If there is nothing particularly memorable about you right now, it is never too early to start working on developing something. Just remember that these things take time and patience.

105
Networking 101

~

Online professional networking has become a powerful tool for growing and managing one's network. There is just as much networking happening online as in person. The days of Rolodexes and Outlook Contacts may be numbered, but you should not rush into discounting them as being old school and ineffective. Why? Maturity levels and the evolution of users of sites like LinkedIn are far from where they should be from the "professional" networking point of view. As the saying goes, "do not put anything in your e-mail that you would not want to put in a letter." Similarly, "do not get into networking unless you are prepared to do it with the highest sprit of professionalism and business relationship." In other words, network online as you would network in person. Furthermore, business relationships get truly developed and cemented in person, not online.

What are the common failures of online networking?

First and foremost, for many individuals online networking is a numbers chase rather than an opportunity to develop quality, functional relationships. The result is large networks that do not work and do not produce the desired results. They lack engagement, knowledge of their members, and relationships with them. How is this different from not having any network at all?

If you really want your *net working* for you, you must get to know people and let them get to know you. This takes time – often months and even years. In the world of thirty-minute solutions to almost anything and limited attention spans, there is no shortcut or magic pill for real networking. People are not invested in helping you if they do not know or respect you and become interested in helping you.

There are also a number of don'ts that you should be aware of. If you understand them, you can establish a network that can truly function to your benefit to generate new business, help in your career growth, or achieve other goals.

Don'ts
- Do not drop impersonal, "built-in" invitation messages to people, asking them to join your network, including to people you actually know, knew, or have not communicated with in

a while. *If you do, what does it tell them?* It says that you are too lazy to take a couple of seconds to type a personal message. It also says that you like spamming people with generic messages and do not care about building a relationship.

- Do not send invitation messages to people you see regularly, without giving them an advance notice, preferably in person. *If you do, what does it tell them?* It says that you do not have the maturity to give them a head's-up that you are sending an invitation. It says that the rote act of adding that individual to your online network list is more important than actually interacting with her or him in person.

- Do not underestimate the simple courtesy of asking if a person would like to join your network or if you can join hers or his. *If you do, what does it say to the other person?* It says that you do not have simple consideration and the respect to check if that individual is interested in connecting with you. Remember that not everybody uses networking tools the same way you do.

- Do not provide recommendations to people and then ask them to do the same. *If you do, what does it tell them?* It shows that people should not take your recommendations seriously. It shows that they simply lack integrity. Recommendations must be professional and appropriate, when the quid pro quo principle is not involved. Otherwise, they are meaningless, likely subjective, and will not be taken seriously by others.

Here are several real-life examples:

- A former colleague of mine, whom I see very often and whom I always *considered* to be a part of my network, sent me an impersonal, standard LinkedIn invitation. This told me that this individual did not respect me enough to ask if I'd be interested in joining her network. She also did not spend a moment to add a personal comment, indicating that she did not care. Regardless of the reasons, I do not want to have such a person in my network.

- A personal acquaintance of mine dropped me an impersonal, standard request to join my business network without asking if I was interested. If he had, I would have told him that I like to keep personal and professional relationships separate. This rule would have excluded him from joining my business network but might have given him the credibility to be added in the future.

- A former acquaintance of mine, whom I barely knew, wrote a glowing recommendation for me and then immediately asked me to write one for her. How can this be taken seriously, and where is the objectivity in this quid pro quo approach?

- Remember that what is modern is the well-forgotten past. The rules for proper networking etiquette are still as relevant as they were fifty years ago, notwithstanding the technology surrounding us. There is something to be said about professionalism and tact in networking, especially in our impersonal, online-based world. The chase after networking numbers may be exciting for a while, but it does not create quality business relationships.

- You must balance quality with quantity. Treat your network members as your business partners, not as numbers in a long list of blind hits. People are barraged with information every day, and they long for relationships with their networks. The numbers game in networking is a fad that will pass. When that happens, do not be left with a large but useless list of contacts. Happy networking!

DISCARD

CPSIA information can be obtained at www.ICGtesting.com
Printed in the USA
LVOW04s0329290815

452025LV00017B/477/P